STEPHEN B. SHEARD

THE FUNNIEST SIDE OF A

DEPRESSED ALCOHOLIC

Copyright © 2009

The right of Stephen Beresford Sheard to be identified as the Author of the Work has been asserted by him in accordance with the Copyright, Designs and Patents Act 1988.

First published in Great Britain in 2009

Apart from any use permitted under UK copyright law, this publication may only be reproduced, stored, or transmitted, in any form, or by any means, with prior permission in writing of the publishers or, in the case of reprographic production, production, in accordance with the licences issued by the copyright Licensing Agency.

WARNING: Contains very strong language and is suitable for those over the age of eighteen only!

This is dedicated to Rosa, my long suffering, beautiful, Latino wife and sons, Daniel and David, the most good looking, talented and personable people on earth. I love them all.

Also dedicated to my mum, Jean, Step-Father, Frank, my sister Pip and my best mates namely:

Ged and Julie Keary

Martin and Christine Jones

Nick and Vanessa Trimble

Sean Brennan, Chris Eavers and Martin Gaw of Kings Ransom / Ransom fame

Thank you for you love, kindness and massive support over the years and in particular over the last terrible six months. You all deserve a medal!!

INDEX

Page

Introduction:	*The First Bit - that nobody reads*	1
Chapter One:	*Birthing Tables and Party Fours*	10
Chapter Two:	*The War Years*	27
Chapter Three:	*Happier Times In Faraway Lands*	47
Chapter Four:	*Back To Very Dark Days*	60
Chapter Five:	*Rock And Roll, Clubs And Balls*	69
Chapter Six:	*Working Life*	84
Chapter Seven:	*Simon's Stories and More*	94
Chapter Eight:	*Odd Things Happen Abroad*	124
Chapter Nine:	*Reflections In The Darkest Of Minds*	148
Chapter Ten:	*My Embarrassment Precedes Me*	173
Chapter Eleven:	*Depression, OCD, Anxiety and*	*198*
	My Black Dog	
Chapter Thirteen:	*So What Do I Do Now?*	272
Chapter Fourteen:	*Finis*	276
Contact Numbers and Help Lines:		277

INTODUCTION:

The First Bit - that nobody reads

All writers are vain, selfish and lazy, and at the very bottom of their motives there lies a mystery – George Orwell.

It seems that there is a direct connection between creative thought and involvement in life and the production of epinephrine by the adrenal gland. When the challenge stops, the supply is turned off; the will to live atrophies – Norman Cousins

'Bollocks!!'

'I'm going to write a book,' I said to my wife Rosa, one sunny August summer evening many years ago. It was one of those balmy evenings when life just seems to slip by, with no worries, no concerns, just peace with the world and everybody and everything in it.

'But you're dyslexic AND a crap typist,' came the response. The chink of the ice in the glass reminded me of the cold chill I felt whenever one of these retorts was made. The gin took hold and another dream drifted into obsolescence...until a year ago.

I was finally sober enough to start.

I'm going to do it, I bloody well am. Sod the doubting Thomases and the disbelievers and my resolve hardened. Walking from the lounge, which housed the icon of quality entertainment, the 32-inch widescreen Phillips with text and additional channels, I rushed through to the back room which housed the computer. This box was slightly older than I was, and almost as weary. Turning it on, I was inspired. Not by the 32-megabyte RAM or the VGA card, but the prospect of my becoming the next Chaucer. I thought for a few moments what this accolade would bring, but then realised that the computer doesn't type s's for f's, (Sucker on the Vicar of Dibley springs to mind!), so that was out. How about Wordsworth? But gardening isn't my strong point and I don't like daffodils!

At this stage the computer decided that it really wasn't up to an hour's work and decided to freeze. Freeze, ice - a gin and tonic! Brilliant! I turned the computer back on and off again and whilst it was booting up, again, with 'gaye' abandon, went to the kitchen for a fill. You will notice that I was already getting into Chaucer and his saucy Wife of Bath habit and was already spelling words with an additional e. Upon my return it was telling me that the fan was working efficiently and windows was booting up.

My thoughts wandered...and wondered some more. The fan was still working, well that's good, and windows is still booting up...and booting up...and booting up. Still, Gordons and Schweppes with ice and a slice! What more could a budding Canterbury Tale-ist want?

How about a bloody computer that worked!

Keep calm Sheardie, keep calm. Coleridge and DeQuinsey were spaced out on opium when they penned their verse not G&T with ice and a slice. I rebooted the computer yet again and sank another mother's ruin and I finally got to the log on screen. What's the password?

'Rosa! What's the password?'

'Dogpoo,' she replied, and with a frown and some consternation, I typed the aforementioned into the crate.

'You have entered a wrong password,' stated the empty box and I bawled back to the Major.

'The password is wrong.'

'Daniel01,' came the response and it was some hours afterwards, once the smell of the culprits bowel emission which decorated the kitchen drifted into the back room, all became clear. The two Cavalier King Charles spaniels which adorned our house would no doubt blame each other and I wasn't going to smell their bottoms to find the culprit.

Typing in the new code, I waited patiently and thought of the day that had passed. I'd given another person the opportunity to become significantly rich. How good was that! What a joy it was to be in a position where I could change lives, to allow people to aspire, to fulfil their dreams, to reach their goals. I was God!

However, God also gave himself an opportunity for a bit

of light relief when he invented the earth and all that went with it. He must have had great fun making light and dark, the heavens and the stars, Adam and Eve etc. The only light relief I had experienced was a sweet corn and tuna sandwich, a sausage roll and some individually hand cooked kettle chips, only just out of date.

Anyway, back to my novel / book/ article/ short story whatever. It's still logging on….and on…..and on…..

Mr Gordon and Mr Schweppes were kind to me that evening keeping me company, and finally Stevenson's Rocket decided to break wind, steamed up, and the screw of Archimedes was turned. However, by now the exciting thought of writing an epic tale was reducing and one where ideas, once so bright, were dulled. I rummaged in grey matter for one good idea to start me off. The word 'War' was slightly shorter than 'Peace' and that would do for the night. By this time I was becoming comatose to the extreme and managed to open a new word document just before I collapsed face first into the keyboard.

Numerous hours elapsed before the General came in looking for her dishevelled foot soldier. 'What on earth are you doing? Wake up you drunken git.' Her compassion and humility was there for all to see and I inebriately responded,

'Writing my first novel!'

'You really are a pillock,' said Rosa as she turned and strode off to the confines of her bed.

I turned to see the screen to see what I had managed to craft prior to my demonic demise. My first book comprised 176,343 letter 'J's where my nose had rested for three and a half hours on the single key. I wonder whether Shakespeare would have been impressed. Still the fan was still working.

That was a year ago and I am now rejuvenated and ready for the task in hand. The computer is still lacking but the brain is eager.

I think everybody wants to write a book! God knows why. It's just one of those things that you want to do when you've either done or tried to do everything else in your life. I either haven't had the opportunity, or the guts, to try to do everything else in life, so that IS bollocks. I've done what I've done and lived as much as I could have. Still typing away in a warm room has its good side.

The difficult thing to decide is what to write about. A novel – I haven't the imagination, a biography- I don't know that much about anybody worth writing about. How about an autobiography?

'Sexual conquests and bed head notches over the last 47 years,' came to mind. 'Writing a very short story, dear?'

So what do I write about? Mmm. How about a tale about a young magician and his many experiences, about his schooling and the adventures which awaited him?

'Bag of shite' as Paul Cooghan used to call it. It would never sell and what would you call the leading character...Harry Potter, best Hairy Squatter!

There's no money in that, it would only appeal to snotty nosed kids who were probably bullied at school and spent more time aiming spot puss using two forefingers at the mirror. God bless the bullied!! My eyes cry a thousand tears thinking of their insufferable pain and anguish and their desperate loneliness; But more of that later.

So, guys and gals, I'm going to write a book about 'Bits and Bobs', This and That, Knickers and Knockers, (Going back to my Les Dawson Days and by the way there are precious few knickers or knockers in this amble).

'You're a pillock, Sheardie, what do you mean 'Bits and Bobs?'

I suppose I mean anything that takes my fancy. I suggest if you like structure, a matriarchal order of things, chapters, plot and sub plot, a beginning and an end, with a twist you nearly saw and can see now quite clearly once you've read it, this rambling wouldn't be for you. I really couldn't give a stuff if it's not kosher, politically correct or the 'done thing'. I probably will be the only one that ever reads it, but no, my lack of methodology, my scattergun approach needs some explanation.

My main preamble, is to recap and reflect on some of

the good things that have happened in my life and in particular the funny things that I have experienced or heard about, and hope that you will enjoy the anecdotes as presented. However, I am a self confessed grumpy old man, a 'miserable tosser of the highest order', and have deep empathy with Victor Meldrew. 'I don't believe it', - I do believe it and it makes me cross.

In my 47 years on this great sphere, one thing quite frankly takes my breath away. How can something so awesome, so incomprehensibly beautiful as this planet, be so shit. War, famine, greed, anger, subversion, manipulation, deceit, the list is quite unending and everybody, *who is anybody*, seems to want to make it worse. A good example is in politics. Every politician that walks the earth, certainly soil laid in Britain, is a complete and utter arse. They pontificate about anything other than the question they were asked and think they are on a different level to the rank and file they represent. For goodness sake, we elected these plonkers to represent us and to make things better. They seem to forget that as soon as they cross the line in parliament.

It makes me a little irate that these parasites appear so early in the book, I thought I would leave their kind to at least chapter 57. Maybe if you are appealed by my challenge to find a new political party, you will enjoy the chapter which includes my manifesto for 'The Common Sense Party'.

So in my ramblings over the next few hundred pages, I may well bang on about anything and spout off about something I'm totally opinionated about. I supposed it's all open to debate. However, this is a book with writing, paragraphs, sentences and letters and I'm the only one who is writing it, so I suppose you'll have to get cross quietly – or write your own book!

Any positive feedback can be posted on high, attached to my web site, forwarded to the publishers. Any negative feedback will not be accepted and will be blocked. Any matters regarding litigation, whether liable issues or otherwise, should be addressed to my solicitor who incidentally died recently.

9

CHAPTER ONE:

Birthing Tables and Party Fours

Relationships are only as alive as the people engaging in them – Donald.B. Ardell

My name is Suzanna Forbes-Heckmondwike and I'm a lady. Well I am on a Saturday and wifey is away. For the rest of the time, my name is Stephen, with a ph, Beresford with an e, Sheard and I'm a middle age man with a middle age spread. I'm not *that* fat - it's containable in an xxl polo shirt.

I have always maintained that I possess a six pack a row of hardened, rippling, stomach muscles that complement my stunning physique and I suppose at one time back in my early twenties, I did. However, with the onset of 'living life to the full and all that goes with it', this was replaced over many years with a Party Four. Any young reader will not know the concept of a Party Four. They haven't lived!

Basically, a Party Four was a huge tin of beer containing four pints of, what can only be described as, fairly shitty beer and was popular at parties in the early seventies. There was also a Party Seven containing, believe it or not, seven pints of fairly shitty beer popular at parties. However, my stomach does not extend to this degree at the present time. Not yet anyway.

You could buy a small tap attached to a contraption which mounted on the top of the huge can. This, via a small gas canister, ejected the gruel-some liquid into the pint pot similar to a pump in a public house. Well that was the selling pitch anyway. Popular as they were, there was a fairly significant design fault with these party somethings, which made for interesting viewing at any teenage party.

Most off-licences sold these mini firkins which tended to be stacked up in the centre of the shop floor as the shelves weren't big enough to accommodate them. So at the age of sixteen, you heard that there was a party at a friend's house and there were going to be some wild chicks there. Donning your best flares, which incidentally had to cover your shoes, and round penny collar, flowery shirt, you would go to the off-licence like a man on a mission. In those days offies tended to sell anything to anyone who looked over twelve.

Waiting outside the shop that had just refused to sell me anything other than some wine gums, I would await my mate who looked fourteen to purchase a Party Four. The biggest problem with it was its size and the fact that it didn't have a handle. This invariably meant that at some stage during the walk to the orgy, the can would slip out of grasp and roll down Cheadle high street, gathering moss and anything else that got in its way.

So you would arrive at the party, lads clutching Party Fours, or if you were really hard, a Party Seven, and the girls with Babysham, Pernot or Martini Rosso, ready for a boozy shag fest. Well, that was the stuff of dreams, wet ones at that, but what you undoubtedly found, was a congregation of 17 lads, three tugs and one pretty filly. Within minutes, seventeen lads would surround the pretty one, who felt so intimidated that she would make her excuses and leave.

So the only thing to do would be to hit the Party Four or Seven and get ratted. However, the beer in these tin containers was so gassy, you could use it to power an F1 fighter jet for three weeks, particularly after the tin had trundled its own way to the party, via the high street. There was real knack of opening these mortar bombs without them exploding; however, it was one skill that I never held an O-Level in. You had to use a can opener, not a traditional one where you removed the whole of the lid, but one which punctured a hole on the top. The bravest amongst the testosterone fuelled stags would go for it. The trouble was that you had to make two holes on opposite sides, one to pour out the revolting contents, and the other to allow air into the container. However, the party house would never have more than one opener.

The gladiator would prepare themselves in full protective gear complete with a plastic rain hat out of his mother's handbag and approach the canister with caution. Then, with a huge gulp of air, trepidation on his face, he would place the opener on the rim and force the metal end through the tin plate. Without fail, a jet of warm, gassy, brown fluid would spurt out of the hole approximately eight to ten feet in the air. This would continue for as long as it took to turn the can around and place another hole on the other side to allow in air. Another strange thing about Party Fours, or Seven if you were 'ard, was that nobody shared them. This is mine and you're not fuckin havin any.

So at the end of the great night, nobody pulled, everyone was pissed and there were seventeen Party Fours lying on the floor, each containing three remaining pints. Also, there were seventeen, six inch brown circles on the ceiling. Those were the days!

So I'm now forty eight and looking twenty years older - goodness me how Party Fours have taken their toll. They used to say I was reasonably good looking, ten and a half stone when I was married in 1984 with blond wavy hair. Now I'm just a typical middle-aged man, almost a TOG, a shaved head, and resemble an old nightclub doorman devoid of steroids or fighting skills. You know, it does creep up on you old age, nature's way of saying you're not here on this planet for long. The fleeting qualities of life are often hard to bear and while most men's mid life crisis paves the way for illicit affairs, a younger model or a motorbike, I'm fuelled with a Jack Daniel induced rock and roll urge to write my first book. I quite fancy a motorbike, though. I might get one of those 500cc Itchy Fannys that are made in Japan.

It's not that I mind being forty eight. It's just as shitty and hard work as being twenty eight, but I think we all feel some injustice that others may have done more in their forty eight years than you have. We are all supposed to be famous for fifteen minutes but in my case I would probably have been infamous had the calling card arrived.

The most depressing thing about it all, and it is said so often it becomes totally boring, but I still think I have the mind of a seventeen year old - have you seen what some of those seventeen year old girls wear on a night out these days - I own bigger hankies. I suppose we have all said it. But is it really true? Everyone has different worries and pressures at every stage of life and as one worry dissipates another one takes its place, as priorities and responsibilities change. As one car sticker once said, I would like to live long enough to be a pain to my kids. The trouble is, I'm starting to be!

It is also so much more difficult for women than men. Ladies are under so much pressure to look younger than they are and present themselves to the best of their ability at all times. This pressure from tabloids, magazines and day television must be stifling and, girls, you have my sympathy. Blokes just have to drag on a pair of jeans and a T-Shirt, whilst the female of the species has to develop the artistic skills of Van Gogh. It's enough to want to make you cut your own ear off.

A good example of coping with life's bite on your bottom was experienced in Centerparcs last year when my family was there with some good friends. This haven of peacefulness and tranquillity was brought to a resounding halt one day when I was in 'The World of Water' with Nick, an equally middle aged man. 'The World of Water' is, to all intents and purposes, a posh swimming pool with slides and whirlpools, waves and potted plants. We were walking having enjoyed the cauldron of the wave pool under a canopy of palm trees, making our way to experience the 'white water rapids' on the upper section of this man made paradise. Knowing I would be showing some skin, I had tried to lose a few pounds before going and to my delight had lost a few ounces. We were walking in our swim shorts, baggy ones not the skin tight Speedos we used to wear - give me some credit. We were clearly full of the joys of spring and enjoying the break from the rigmarole and stress of everyday life.

As we walked, we passed a couple of young lads probably around fourteen years old. They seemed to be also enjoying the experience and were laughing and joking. When they were approximately five yards behind us, I heard one of them say to the other,

'Did you see the size of the tits on that?'

Both Nick and I looked around to see the fit beauty with the 38DD cups they were referring to. However, we were the only four people in sight. Both Nick and I did wait until they were out of sight before we looked down at our cleavage. We quickly realised that we know what our own breasts look like, but had not really taken the time to study each others. We studied each others. To this day, I am convinced that they were talking about Nick's and not mine. Nick thinks it's the other way around. By the way, if ever you meet Nick, become friends and want to give him a present he wears a 42 inch FF cup and prefers Gossard.

Anyway, I digress.

It was the 24th June 1960 and I was practising my front

crawl. The water was warm and inviting. My fingers and toes, once webbed, had little effect against the tide and I didn't seem to be going anywhere, just drifting. I was desperate to become the youngest child ever to be awarded the twenty five metres length certificate and changed to back stroke and attempted to swim with the tide rather than against it. However, I was tied by a rope around my waist attached to the pool side, and I decided to rest. I know you shouldn't fall asleep in water as it's dangerous, but I was weary and it hadn't done me any harm so far. The regular beat of the heating pump coaxed me to sleep, rhythmic and pulsating.

Suddenly, I awoke with a start. The pool began to empty, slowly at first then an almighty gushing sound filled my ears and the water around me was suddenly no more. As it disappeared, my head, with the pressure, was forced into the plug hole at the bottom of the pool. The hole was only tiny and I couldn't understand what was forcing me towards it. I was mortified by the noise and changes around me - I must be dying.

Over the next few hours time passed so slowly. I was petrified by this new experience, desperate to return to the warm and inviting water that had left me behind. The hole appeared to be getting larger and larger, revealing a long tunnel and my head was jamming further and further into it. All I wanted to do was to swim again. However, I was not to do that again for many years. The pressure was becoming unbearable as my whole head was forced into the dark black well, soon, I was sure, it would explode. This was like my worst nightmare, and probably would have been if I had learned to dream.

Suddenly, cold air chilled my bald head and the tunnel in which I had been forced through expanded to accommodate. 'What the bloody hell is going on?' I thought, as my forehead caught the chill and bloody secretions were dragged across my face by the rubber latex that retained me. 'The Force' pushed me further and further with no chance of retreat. The air hit my face and I opened my eyes, blinded by the light, strangled by the restraint that was now constricting my neck. 'I am dying!' I cried although no sound passed my lips.

Abruptly, the rest of my body ejected out of the grip and I was free, but free into what? The sight that confronted me looked frightening and I was confused, bewildered, petrified. Huge fingers grabbed at me but also offered some comfort and I slowly relaxed, comforted by the warmth and texture of the skin that caressed me.

Whack. It then smacked my arse with a sound of a butcher tenderising the toughest of Aberdeen Angus top-side. I began to wail. I hadn't died, I'd been born!

And in many ways I have been confused, bewildered and petrified ever since and have certainly never stopped wailing during bottom slapping or any other event for that matter.

I was born in Withington Hospital in Manchester. Bit of a shit time to be born, really. Far too young to enjoy the decadent, swinging, free love, sixties and you know you would turn forty in the year 2000. My parents had humble upbringings. Gordon, an only child, was raised in Holmfirth in Huddersfield to a choir master / piano teacher and his wife, who was the most rotund woman ever to walk the planet. As a youngster, I remember Dad, my sister Pip and I would drive over to visit her in Huddersfield now and again on a Saturday morning. Whilst her house would now be described as a quaint Victorian property with many original features, it truly was a dusty, dirty, grotty house that needed gutting.

She lived on her own as my granddad had died many years before at the age of 57 from a heart attack. She was huge, a tiny pint pot in height but was alleged to have a waist the same number of inches as her stature. Whilst Dad attempted to find a clean enough frying pan to cook some smoky bacon for lunch, I would always go into the 'study' to play on an old pedal pump organ which had 20 stops to change the tone and pitch of the notes. The old groaner must have been used to teach music to the music teacher's pupils, and invariably I would have to mend the material ties that attached the foot pumps to the bellows. Those were the days.

We would always go to the match afterwards to watch beloved Huddersfield Town and would stand watching Frank Worthington out of the Cow Shed, hoping that we would win the golden goal competition.

On one match day we approached the ground and I was approached by a photographer and a reporter for the Huddersfield Gazette.

' How doo! Wer dooin an article on why people still come t' Town and how far people travel.'

Well it was a real coup. We travelled a one hundred mile round trip to go to t' Town and they loved it. I had made myself a rattle following the instructions in my Shoot magazine. I think rattles are now banned for safety reasons but mine was legal and proudly bore Huddersfield colours of blue and white. Wrapped in a scarf, the photographer snapped away and details were taken from my dad about where we lived etc. A week later the article appeared and a paper was sent to our house by the printers for the scrap book.

The picture and content were excellent, however, I noticed that on my rattle I had printed in bold lettering, 'Hudersfield 'R' Ace'. On noticing my error when sign writing, I had appended an extra D with an inflection. I must have been the laughing stock of Yorkshire. He has supported the blues all his life and he can't even spell the Town's name. Where does he come from Dyslexishire? What a pillock!

My mother, Jean, was born in the hardy farming community in Kirby Stephen in Cumbria. Her father was a train driver all his life and was in a reserved occupation transporting goods in the Second World War. I recall he had two thumbs and only seven and a half fingers. The little finger on his left hand had been squashed between two buffers connecting carriages on his train. Somewhat painful, I would suggest.

He was a gentle man, unlike my grandmother, who was

fairly formidable. At some stage they moved to Blackpool and we used to have the occasional day out to visit them. My main memories of Blackpool are few and grainy. (That's grainy not rainy). I always remember, Barton Bridge over the Manchester Ship Canal and the white windmill just outside St Annes from the journey. Both signified that you were nearly there, or nowhere near there, depending on which way you were travelling. I also remember an old clock in my Granny's house, no idea why. We always used to visit the pier to play the slotties. I once found one that paid out every time you started the cherries rolling and with so many tuppences weighing down my pockets, I could hardly walk.

I also remember the laughing clown in a glass box on the Pleasure Beach. The clown had to be one of the scariest things I had ever seen and it was sited adjacent to the 'House of Horrors' which was the second. I thought you went to the Pleasure Beach for 'pleasure', not to be scared witless. The laughing clown was supposed to make you laugh. It just made me fill my pants.

My parents met at Manchester University where Gordon studied Chemistry and Jean, English. Following a number of early placements and training years, Dad ended up working at Clayton Aniline Company, a dyestuffs manufacturer, which was later sold to Ciba Geigi. Initially he was a research chemist studying dye stuffs for the textile and food stuffs industries.

'Never eat any blue food,' I remember him once telling

me. Quite interesting to hear of the demise of the blue Smartie some years ago, albeit, I gather it is now back on the shelves or certainly in the tubes on the shelves. By the way did you know you can make a Smartie tube into a rocket launcher and fire the coloured end approximately three feet. I wonder if those coloured end caps still have a letter printed on the underneath? I digress!

His factory was one of the most awe-inspiring places I have ever visited. To put it in context and give you an idea of the size, it had its own fire station with full time firemen and covered acres and acres. Every year there would be an open day where relatives and friends could visit and I remember those trips vividly. The pipes and vats and steam and smells created a cacophony to the senses and I loved visiting the laboratory where my Dad mixed coloured concoctions, blasting them in heat and cold and whizzing them in centrifuges. I sometimes wonder whether he ever whizzed me in the machine I am so mixed up. At least my blood is red and not blue.

My Mum, following an some years at Levenshulme High for Girls, landed a job at one of Manchester's finest Independent schools, namely, Manchester High School for Girls teaching English and English Literature. She had a passion for all the great authors and was obviously inspired by her subject. Every year she took on an extra responsibility marking 'O' level papers for the Joint Matriculation Board. Some of you will remember it as the JMB. She progressed to be a Senior Examiner, standardising other markers and finally was asked to become Assistant Chief Examiner, where she helped the Chief Examiner set the 'O' level paper. So if you failed English Literature in the mid seventies, you can blame my mum. I passed it with an A, and no she didn't help me.

The first four years of my life we lived in a semi-detached house in Didsbury. Apparently, I never stopped crying, a trait that would continue the rest of my life. I was obviously an emotional little thing. Either that or I filled my nappy constantly, a trait that would also continue the rest of my life. I can remember little up to four years of age other than standing against a brick wall of a nearby house and daddy-long-legs crawled onto my neck. I was scared witless and still struggle to this day accepting moths and large flying insects as an acceptable part of God's creation.

I schooled from infancy at Didsbury Church of England Primary School on Elm Grove, opposite the old picture house which accommodated my sister and me every Saturday afternoon matinee. Like life, everything was black and white in those days, Flash Gordon, Tonto, Skippy, Buck Rogers. And another thing, we never stuffed our faces with popcorn and Kiora. You were lucky to be treated to a choc-ice from the lady with the torch. The picture house was closed down as did many of the smaller cinemas, or flea pits, as we used to call them. A Bingo hall was created, quickly to fail, and a number of years ago fell into the hand of developers who converted the lot into duplex apartments. It's quite sad really.

'Which apartment do you live in?'

'Oh, two little ducks, twenty two!'

'I'm in one fat lady! Have you seen the state of the man who hangs around Kelly's eye?'

The school was imposing and bleak. Victorian in architecture, it boasted high walls around its perimeter, classroom ceilings that went on forever, and sash windows that were operated with a cord. The whole school smelled of cauliflower, wee and cleaning fluid. The atmosphere was dour and fairly regimented, with the strap being administered across the hand for minor misdemeanours.

I looked in my early days like the milky bar kid (without the glasses) with a shock of blond, almost white hair, and was fairly small for my age. No! I was the milky bar kid! Strong and tough and only the best was good enough, the creamiest milk, the whitest bar, the goodness that's in Milky Bar.

I remember in infants pooing my pants one day, during a French lesson. What on earth were we being taught French at that age for? Half the kids in the class couldn't speak a word of English. Actually, did I soil my pants in infants or was it at the petrol station whilst filling my car the other day? No it was definitely in infants. I had tried and tried to last out as the French teacher was a complete and utter bitch and wouldn't have let me go to the toilet even if I had asked.

I had to stand in an open corridor with no trousers or underpants, as children, teachers, paedophiles and visitors to the school, ***philed*** past. (This isn't a spelling mistake; it's a play on words!) There was no place to hide my indignity. There was no screen or alcove in the wall to cower. I can still remember shaking with the self loathing and embarrassment of it all. The upset this enforced flashing had on me was vast, only to continue when the teacher provided me with a replacement pair of trousers. These were red tailored shorts with a red bib and two straps that went over the shoulders, fastening at the back. For the afternoon, I walked around the playground looking like the leader of an Austrian UmPah band. The lederhosen are on me boys!

This degradation and total lack of humility brought on by an unsympathetic, uncaring cow of a woman, typified what was to happen to me on a number of occasions in my younger days. Indignity continued to spread through teenage years and to an extent must have affected me all my life, one way or another. I certainly, not for one minute, think that I have suffered more than most. Far from it! Many will think that I have been incredibly lucky in my upbringing, almost born with a silver spoon in my mouth. However, it is ***how*** one deals with certain events in life and certainly how ***well*** one deals. Pragmatism has never been my strong point and if anything is half worth worrying about, I would worry about it for months. If I didn't worry about something, I would worry whether I should be worrying about not worrying about something.

We moved to Cheadle Hulme in 1964 to a large four bedroom detached property with 1/3rd of an acre gardens. This was heaven and provided a comfortable and happy home for many years. My mum drove me to school every morning the four miles, and the traffic was always very busy. I can remember, every day upon leaving, she would open a packet of Nuttall's Mintoes and whilst we were stuck in the traffic, we would suck the sweet hoping to make it last longer than the other. Caring as she was, dentistry was not her subject at University and she still cannot understand why I needed so many fillings. I don't have any teeth, no, just amalgam and I was a role model for Jaws in the famous James Bond movie, the name of which escapes me.

I quite enjoyed Junior school and have little memory of any particular events other than I had several girlfriends. Well, they aren't girlfriends really are they? I do remember kiss and chase where the girls would run after the boys to try to kiss them. One girl once followed me into the brick toilets in the playground. You've never seen me run out of anywhere so fast in my life! She had a face like melted Wellington boot.

Another thing the girls used to do was take their knickers off and do cartwheels! How bizarre is that? One of my chat up lines later in life was, 'Have you ever taken your knickers off and done a cartwheel?' No wonder I always came out of clubs with my right cheek far redder than the left.

I once won an award for the most pogo jumps without falling off. It was over 100, no mean feat. I also once had a fight, and won. I pushed him harder than he pushed me. It just shows how little goes on in life on occasions if all that one can remember in the first ten years is pogo sticks, one fight and naked cartwheels.

It's funny, but remembering back to those days, it's hard to remember anything other than long balmy summer evenings, listening to Dad cut the grass as I lay awake in bed wondering why I couldn't stay up. After all it was still daylight. Or Christmas when everything was magical, the days leading up to the 25th had an air of expectancy and excitement. Happy times, happy times, the innocence of youth and when time passed incredibly slowly. We had no worries, no responsibilities and nothing to live for other than life itself, which on the whole was great. How things would deteriorate over the next decade.

CHAPTER TWO:

The War Years

When we think of cruelty, we must try to remember the stupidity, the envy, the frustration from which it has arisen – Edith Sitwell

In this world everything changes except good deeds and bad deeds; these follow you as the shadows follow the body – Ruth Benedict

Turning eleven, I had the world in front of me. I had 'graduated' to an independent school, however, I chose, due to the distance and potential daily journey, to forgo my place and go to the local Grammar school. Unbeknown to me, Cheadle Moseley Grammar School for Boys should more appropriately have been named Cheadle Moseley Borstal for Nutters and Bullies, as I was to find out. I was to hear many years later that the Deputy Head Master, nicknamed 'Growler', stated that my intake year was the worst behaved and unruly year he had ever experienced in forty years of teaching.

I entered this living torment in September 1971, full of zest for life and eager to learn. I loved the variation in the education provided and the fact that you had different teachers for different subjects. I studied reasonably well in the first two years and thoroughly enjoyed the challenge, taking pride in whatever I was asked to achieve. The only caveat to this, was my complete and utter fear of one particular teacher, and interestingly it was in a subject that I would later spend a great deal of my life pursuing….Music.

On the third day of my schooling, all the classes had been set and we were starting to learn our way around the school. The fifth period of the seven period day was Music and we all lined up outside the music room. The teacher swept by in a gown and black mortar, a thunderous look on his face, screaming at us to get in and sit down. His name was Parker, commonly known as Pinky Parker and has a face cross between, Sir Andrew Lloyd Webber and Liberace. He apparently had a different bow tie for every day of the year and he always had a whisky in his coffee first thing in the morning.

On that first lesson, he sat at his desk, his head puce with anger, for what reason, who knows, who cares, he was demonic. He commenced compiling his register.

'Who's first in alphabetical order?' he erupted. No one had any idea. We had only known each other for two days.

'WHO IS FIRST in alphabetical order? **Speak!**' the enraged musical director spluttered.

'Andrews, Sir.'

'Christian name?'

'Peter.'

'**Peter, Sir!**' he screamed. '**NEXT!**'

Total panic broke out and all the class whispered to each other, desperate to respond correctly. He allowed this for a few seconds. Maybe Pinky did have a heart.

'**NEXT.**'

This continued over and over again throughout the early alphabet letters and it was slowly coming to the S's.

'Shepherd, Sir.'

'Christian name?'

'Christopher, Sir.'

'Next.'

'Sheard, Sir.'

Those in the class clever enough to know that Sheard should have come before Shepherd, gasped. The one boy in question looked highly embarrassed.

'Come here Sheard!' and he walked towards his stock room which housed the instruments and music stands and instruments of gratuitous pain and discomfort. 'Stand there.' He pointed just outside the door, and disappeared into the room, his gown dancing in the slip stream.

He came out with an adult plimsoll. A white pump to us oldies, a soft trainer shoe to you upstarts.

'Bend over!" he ranted and whacked my brand new school trousers hard against my pimply bottom.

'Get it right from now on!'

What a delightful chap he was! I can honestly say that I couldn't sleep on a Tuesday night for months, fearful of what might happen in Music.

There was also a sinister side to the man. He certainly had his favourites and he used to ask them to join him on his piano stool to engage in a little fortissimo around the ivories. I even recall, one lad once sat on his knee to play a duet. That was certainly some movement!

Alas, I have heard that Pinky died a number of years ago. Six foot under or sitting on the top of a mantelpiece is probably the best place for him. Long may he suffer in purgatory.

The first two years of secondary school I just about survived. There were constant fights on the quad, where all the stags vied for the premier spot, constant victimisation of anyone who appeared to be anything other than a mini Rocky and constant reminders that we were living in an age where adults i.e. teachers, could beat or hit young children at will. Still - this was a grammar school, a provider of quality education.

In third year, things turned for the worse. I had learned from my experiences in the school, that one shouldn't be seen to try too hard at anything other than football. This was a severe weakness and punishable by death. Well not quite but at times it would have been a preferred route. It didn't help that I was always crap at football and certainly hate the game and everything it stands for these days. It's a great game in itself. It's just a shame it is played by utter vain, preening, self important, loathsome, over-paid, demi-gods, worshipped by obsessed, tribal, blinkered low lifes. There we are! Let's get the party started. The first section of the community that will be following me are football fans and they will undoubtedly have revenge in mind.

I was in one of the top sets, but had not done quite as well in some exams as I would have hoped. Actually, I couldn't give a shit by this stage, but my mum and dad were a bit disappointed. The re-structuring as we went into third year meant that we were re-assessed on these exams, and I was placed in a different class, a "mixed ability' class. The class constituted my pal, Simon, who went on to become my best man, me, and twenty eight thugs whose only mixed ability was the severity of thrashing they could impart. I'm being a little unfair to my classmates here. There weren't twenty eight thugs. I supposed it just seemed like it. There were probably eight. However, the fear and intimidation that they created made the other twenty pale into insignificance.

I suffered from bad psoriasis on my scalp as a youngster and in one lesson a teacher tapped me on my head for some misdemeanor. As a result, he transferred a lump of coal tar cream onto his fingers.

'What's this?' he shouted.

I told him that it was cream for my condition. 'So it's for your scabby head is it?' came the retort. From that day onwards for possibly eighteen months I was known by all the pupils as Scabhead.

One of the favourite pastimes of the Core of Eight was to call a 'bash'. A bash had all the hallmarks of a beating and undertaken anyone who could be bothered to join in. Whilst a bash was not full on, it still involved approximately twelve kids kicking, hitting and thumping you all over, as you cowered in fetal position for sixty seconds or so. Whether the lads were fond of my nickname or just hated my guts, a Scabhead bash was a very common occurrence, possibly every other day. Whilst blood was rarely drawn, the real marks stayed for a lifetime and I can even now identify why I am like I am in certain confrontational situations. In many respects, it wasn't the beating, but the fear of one. For example, in one chemistry lesson, I was advised at the beginning of the lesson via a note that had gone around everyone else first, that there would be a 'Scabhead' bash at the end of the lesson. Telling the teacher was just not an option. It would be suicide.

Those forty minutes were, quite honestly unbearable. How it must feel, as a condemned man to count the minutes away to your execution, I just cannot imagine.

When the forty minutes was up and the teacher left the room, all and sundry piled in, all attempting to leave a piece of themselves on me. I don't know whether the wait has increased additional testosterone but they went for it a little more enthusiastically than usual. When it was over they dispersed and I cried.

I don't know why really. It's funny. When you are being kicked and hit so many times at once, it doesn't really hurt. I suppose the body can only deal with one hurt at a time.

Another variation on a theme was the selection of two boys out of the class to have a fight. If they didn't have a fight, they would both be beaten. How can you have a fight with someone who has done you no harm and neither of you were that way inclined anyway.

Every waking minute in the third year, now known as year nine, was purgatory. How many nights did I lie crying in bed worrying about the following day? I know how children have committed suicide as a result of bullying and you occasionally read these horrific stories in the press. If you are bullied you can tell no one, not your parents, the teachers and your friends already know. All you believe is that if it comes out that you have squealed, you would have your head kicked in. So what do you do? You live with it and hope that one day it will go away. Being beaten isn't anywhere near as hurtful or harmful as the thought of being beaten. That may sound strange, however, it is the anxiety and fear of when it will happen again that creates the long term damage. Upon reflection of my life thus far, I am convinced that the psychological torture and abuse endured at school has affected me every day in some respect.

I hate crowded places and noisy pubs and bars. I feel

very uncomfortable walking into some places and networking whereby you walk into a roomful of people and start to chat about business matters etc. fills me with dread. Later in life, I developed Obsessive Compulsive Disorder (OCD) concerning parties in and around where I lived. I would look out of a bedroom window up to 40 times per night, particularly on a Saturday night to see if any of the neighbours were partying. If they even had an extra car at the house I would have a major panic and anxiety attack and drink myself into unconsciousness. I have no doubt that some of the goings on at school during that period, have had a major effect on my depressive tendencies, anxiety and panic attacks and obssessiveness for the rest of my life.

One particular day was most dreaded at school. The day you were supposed to look forward to all year was the one that you most feared, your birthday.

'Scabhead, happy birthday,' the eight said in unison. Please accept this gift of book tokens and this hand decorated chocolate sponge with contrasting candles as our gesture of tidings for this wondrous day. As you can guess, rather to the contrary.

A wave of new invention had been bestowed on the eight that year and one had contrived the ordeal of toilet ducking. This constituted the lowering of birthday boy's head deep into the pan of the toilet and flushing the cistern to wash the boy clean. In my particular case, this baptism was performed every day for the first eight days of my fourteenth year of life on this planet. The bazaar thing about this was that you would walk around for the next hour with wet hair and everyone you met said 'Happy Birthday.'

I have thought about tracking the eight down via 'Friends Re-United', not to rekindle my contact with them and discuss our happy schooldays, but to systematically kill each and every one of them. Of course this would not be quick and would involve chloroform, gaffer tape, my prized Bosch rechargeable drill and an assortment of interchangeable drill bits. I think I would start with a 3mm wood bit through each of the fingernails. Ultimately they would each end up a human colander and of course this would be done over a period of, say eight days, to match the number of toilet ducks.

Another particular regular event included being nutted on the back of the head from behind when you were totally unaware that anyone was there. The 'happy slapper', the modern day shits from hell, really are doing nothing new. The only thing they do different is have the ability to be able to film their misdemeanour on the mobile phone they stole that morning. If I had my way, anyone found with a happy slapping snippet on their phone would have the offending telephone inserted into their anal orifice with the vibrate ring tone on.

The nutting offences mostly took place in lessons when the teacher's back was turned and was particularly popular in chemistry and physics where pupils were mobile around the class room undertaking 'experiments'.

There were some very interesting 'experiments' undertaken, particularly in chemistry, where the teacher, who was in his forties, had come late into the profession thinking that it would be less demanding. Unfortunately, his discipline was weak to say the least and it took probably less than twenty minutes for the kids to pick up on this. One lad actually lit up a fag at the back of one of his lessons and passed it around. The next year of this teacher's life was hell and he left soon after having suffered a nervous breakdown.

Giving the scumbags water, gas, acid and fire to play with for 40 minutes was like inviting Bin Laden to do some target practice with a Browning in a Christian maternity ward. Pupils regularly walked out of the lesson with only three quarters of a school jacket. The other quarter had been subject to an experiment as to whether acid or fire had more destructive qualities on cloth.

Another favourite was to take a plastic hose and attach one end to the gas pipe which fed the bunsen burners and the other end to the water tap, turning them both on simultaneously. The experiment was to determine which utility supplier had the more pressure, gas or water. A number of the local residents in houses on North Downs Road, the street leading up to the school, were able to enjoy the findings, when they attempted to cook tea that evening when water came out of their cookers.

'Anyone for a boil in a bag meal?'

Another amazingly crazy act outside the classroom was

down in the bike sheds. One or more kids on regular occasions, decided to either remove or loosen the nuts holding on the front wheels of all the bikes in the rack. Bear in mind that the first the owners knew about the off-beat engineering work undertaken on their machines, was at the end of North Downs Road, where it met a very busy main road. At most schools the conversation would go, 'Have you got some ciggies? Great, let's go to the bike shed.'

In our school it was, 'Have you any 15mm torque wrenches on you? Great, let's go to the bike shed.'

I wasn't the only one to be bullied severely. I remember one lad in the third year who was slightly effeminate. One day at lunch time on the quad (the playground) he was standing on his own some thirty feet away from a marauding gang. He was on the grass adjoining the quad and on the other side of a full steam train track which was a project of one of the teachers. The school was famous for having this facility with train rides and a society for those who were interested. In between the sleepers was aggregate comprising one inch limestone. The gang had armed themselves with handful of these weapons and were literally stoning the young boy. Truly heartbreaking and I am sure his mind has been affected ever since.

Teachers weren't exempt from the express attack both mentally and physically from these 'grammar' school children, whose actions and audaciousness on occasion beggared belief.

One history teacher, a female, bore the majority of the brunt of misfortune. Once again she had no control whatsoever over her charges and I really feel for her knowing what she went through. On one occasion, she was away from the teacher's desk which supported her bag, assisting a pupil. Four of the other boys in her charge, placed one house brick each in her briefcase which they had smuggled into class in their bags. The clasp of the teacher's case was fastened and it was only at the end of the lesson and all had left that she realized that she was carrying far more books to mark that night than she thought.

Testicles and penises were drawn on her plastic belt whilst she was leaning over away from another crazed hoodlum one day. I cannot imagine how she felt when she walked into the staff room and it was pointed out to her that someone had practiced erotic art on her apparel. Another thoughtless tosser taking away another being's dignity.

Possibly the worst case was that of a normally respectable pupil with whom I was friendly. Totally out of character one day, he decided to remove every nut and bolt and dowel out of a classroom chair. This was then placed behind the teacher's desk. For all intense and purposes, the chair stood beautifully and looked like any other chair.

I remember the teacher in question as he taught me A Level English. Well, he didn't actually teach me A Level English. All he did for two years was translate the Olde English version of Chaucer's Cantebury Tales into modern English, making us write it down word for word. In actual fact you could go to a local bookshop and purchase the full translated version. One reason for his apparent lack of motivation for the subject he taught was probably due to his inebriated state every afternoon, following the consumption of five pints every lunch hour at the Kenilworth pub down the road.

Anyway, this teacher arrived for the lesson, the first lesson post lunch, and sat down on the chair which promptly fragmented. The poor drunk was able to allocate additional time every morning to consume his favourite beverage over the next seven months. This was the length of his sick note for a slipped disc. The boy was allocated six strokes of the cane on his behind and suspended for two days.

The purgatory called Secondary School finally started to dissipate when I was in Year 5 (now called Year 11). By this stage, I had realized that the only way to gain any respect from the mob was to be seen to be non-compliant with the 'supposed' strict regime of the school. I therefore started to become a rather "naughty" boy. In my 'O' Level year, I was involved in a numerous incidents which resulted in a number of disciplinary procedures.

I was caught smoking at smoker's corner by a teacher who smoked 40, No. 6 cigarettes a day. No. 6 fags incidentally cost 21p for 10 whilst dinner money was 20p. It was a daily decision as to whether to indulge in the culinary delights hidden in the school canteen, or bunk off to the local shop to buy 10. Having said that, one had to find 1p on the street walking to the shops, or ask the purveyor of this rough tobacco to split a packet and sell you 5 at a hefty profit to him.

I digress! A number of us were marched into the Deputy Headmaster's office to be told that a letter would be sent to our respective parents to advise them of our misdemeanour and that we were to attend a number of detentions. Whilst the detentions were completed over the next few days, three days after being caught, we had a sacrificial burning of the letters at smoker's corner, the letters having been intercepted on the front door mat at home. One has to remember that in those days we did have a semblance of a postal service and letters would be delivered the same time every morning and afternoon.

I was also involved in poker and brag card schools which took place virtually at any time or place and was caught on a number of occasions. I also won on a couple of occasions!

As my behaviour deteriorated, my parents became a little concerned to say the least. As a result I was placed on 'Report' which basically means that I had to have a card signed at every lesson, primarily to confirm that I had attended, and secondly to advise whether I had been a good boy or not. What complete and utter tosh.

I ultimately struggled to achieve 6, A-C grades, which delighted everyone. I couldn't believe it, I'd only sat 5. That's not true actually, I had sat 8 and the two I failed were french and chemistry. Failing chemistry was particularly disappointing for my dad considering he was a research chemist but, Hey Ho! When I first received the certificates through the post I actually I thought that I had passed these two subjects as well.

I remember so clearly opening the envelope to receive my results. I scanned down the subjects and for French I was awarded a U and the same for Chemistry. Unbelievably good, Undoubtedly brilliant, Unequivocally stupendous. Neither of these, I afraid- Unclassified.

I went on to study three A levels, but my heart was never in it and combined with appalling teaching, went on to fail all of them. My mum, in her capacity as Assistant Chief Examiner of English at the JMB, has always stated that to have only been set two essays in two years on an A Level English course, beggared belief. However, I quite enjoyed 6th form, both lower and upper. All the yobs had either left or grown up sufficiently to realise the error of their ways and bullying no longer remained a problem. However, I was still immature and rather naughty considering I was almost a man, and I suppose this immaturity has followed me through life in general.

I was the first ever 6th former to be banned from the 6th form common room for vaulting a work station desk unit only to land on the deputy Headmaster's foot and was confined to the canteen for free periods for three months.

However, I was also first in an area which gave me

some credibility amongst my peers. Simon, my future best man and I joined the debating society, a weekly event after school on a Wednesday. Yes, I know it sounds more akin to University Challenge than rock and roll. However, there was a particular reason for this.

Adjoining our school was the girl's school and attached to the main building was a pre-fabricated unit which housed the girl's common room. The debating society was held in this building and the debate took place almost as a competition between the girls and the boys. I think we went twice and I cannot recall what the debates were about. In actual fact, even as we were **leaving** on both occasions, I didn't know what the debates were about.

What it did allow us to do was to get to know some of the young fillies from the girly school. We also learned that it was allowed but never practised, that the 6th form boys from the boy's school could actually go into the girl's 6th form common room at lunch times. Nobody had ever done this. Either they did not know they could, or they did not have the bottle to do it. Well Simon and I knew and Simon and I had the bottle to do it.

For approximately eighteen months of my two years in 6th form, every lunch time, Simon and I sat in a room with around one hundred females. Top bombing I would say and helped me develop many social skills, inter-personal skills and the ability to undo a girl's bra exceedingly quickly with one hand, either left or right, a feat I am still adept at, but rarely have the chance to practise.

Throughout my schooling, sport played a large part, in particular tennis and I actually represented or participated at a reasonable level in eight different sports albeit, the length of the total appearance time representing the school varies considerably. Football – for one half of one match, Hockey – two matches, Table Tennis – One Inter Schools Competition, Rugby – Hooker for one match, Gymnastics (was at one time able to do a round off, double flick flack, open back somersault), Trampolining – high spot was full twisting double back somersault (I can still do an open back somersault at the age of 49 on the trampoline in the back garden) and Tennis – Stockport Schools Champion and represented Cheshire at Junior and Senior level.

The only other thing I used to love during those years was the television. My favourite program was The New Avengers with Purdie. Joanna Lumley was my heart throb for many a year even though she was considerably older and I would watch late night episodes until the early hours just for the sight of a suspender belt. Morecombe and Wise, The Two Ronnies, Blue Peter, Debbie Does Dallas were some of my other favorites. It may sound a little strange, and I imagine that you wouldn't expect anything else of me now that you have read the first few chapters, but I used to love the adverts.

One of my favourite ever TV commercials many years ago, featured a man placing his card into an ATM and out popped a toffee crisp wrapper. I have to say that this was marginally beaten by the Shake and Vac advert, as I used to fancy the woman who was doing her vacuuming particularly when she spun and her skirt flew up as she shook the cleaning solution onto the unsuspecting fleas on the carpet. I did find her so attractive that she formed the erotic image in many a ham shank. "You do the Shake and Vac and put the freshness back, it's all you have to doooo", she used to wail. She could have shaked and vacced me and put the freshness back anytime she wanted.

The only other contender that I can think of was the young man who wasn't up to doing his exams today because his nose was blocked up with a cold.

'Try this Malcolm,' she insisted, in a forceful yet consoling manner, handing him a tube of Sinex comforting him in the knowledge that it lasted eight hours.

'Eight hours.'

'So how did it go, Malcolm?'

'The Sinex, never used it once mum.'

'No! The exam silly.'

I only ever used Sinex once squirting the tube of Hell's brimstone up my nose and at the same time sniffing as hard as I could. It was like firing a steel bolt into my forehead through the nasal channel, never to be attempted again. So if you want to feel like the local nag on death's row at the knackers yard, try some Sinex. It'll blow your mind.

I also tried a product called Contact 3000 a number of years ago which too, was supposed to dry up colds. It actually turned the mucus into blood i.e. a nose bleed. It started at Manchester airport as we were heading to the Italian Alps, skiing in Courmayeur. The nose bleed lasted whilst we were on the plane, the coach, all through the first night and all day the second day. At this stage I was losing so much blood that it was decided to ship me off to the local hospital. Never mind Tony Hancock and his blood donor sketch, I wasn't giving up an arm full, I was giving up a body's worth.

We were holidaying with four Doctors and they stated that I would have it cauterised. I didn't. I had it packed with two tampons the size of bath towels which went all the way up the nose and down into the adenoids. It was a pretty revolting experience, particularly when they came to remove the offending articles.

The only other time I was in so much pain from something that was supposed to help me was when my sister Pip told me that if you had a spot, putting perfume on it, helped the spot dry up. One day, when I was around 12, I caught my John Thomas in the zip of my flies making a small incision. (That was my story and I'm sticking to it!)

'I wonder if that remedy Pip told me about would help restore John to his former glory?' I thought to myself. Out came the Brut. 'Splash it all over, Harry,' as Frank Bruno used to say on the advert. This was duly done. I can honestly say that the indescribable pain endured over the next nine minutes has had a major effect on my long term mental state. 'Why nine minutes?' I hear you cry. Well it took me that long to get to the bathroom to wash it off. Have you ever seen a human moving along a landing like a caterpillar? I have!

No longer can I look at a bottle of Brut aftershave and avoid going to places where it might be on display. Even the application of Old Spice requires gas and air obtained from a friendly and errant midwife. I have also been sectioned under the mental health act on three separate occasions when I have heard the Jerry Lee Lewis song, 'Great balls of fire' on the radio.

CHAPTER THREE:

Happier Times In Faraway Lands

Happiness is the meaning and the purpose of life, the whole aim and end of human existence - Aristotle

I have enjoyed many holidays in my life and whilst being the nervous type that is always apprehensive and totally obsessive about the safety of the accommodation and location, always look forward to the experience. Whilst not particularly well travelled, certainly compared to the many students who take a year out to travel the world (they really are lucky bastards aren't they?), I have had the good fortune to travel on many foreign vacations throughout my life albeit not until I was old enough to go without family.

Early holidays with my family were always in the UK and nearly always on the south coast as my father would not fly. The only time I went abroad was when I was eleven and involved a coach trip to sunny Ostend and the delights and attractions of Belgium. The holiday was incredibly boring but as an eleven year old I did make friends with a number of old age pensioners. I could not, however, enjoy the delights of Stella Artois and also did not meet Poirot.

Devon and Cornwall were the favourite destinations for our one week away from it all and we spent many happy years on holidays in places such as Torbay, Ilfracombe and Bournemouth. We always drove, setting off very early in the morning, always ate the sweets we had bought the previous day within the first hour and always had to turn back to make sure that the gas oven was off.

Maybe this obsessive behaviour has been handed down genetically, as I have suffered from Compulsive Obsessive Disorder most of my life in one form or other. I also remember that we always used to buy pear drops, the smell of which made my dad physically heave.

I remember my first ever kiss was at the Lee Bay Hotel in Ilfracombe with a girl who was a year older than I was, a trait I was to develop and maintain pretty well throughout my life, dating and marrying older women. My leaning towards older women has always intrigued me and I wonder whether it was a result of being so pathetically soft, gentle and needing someone to guide, assure and lead me through my troubled life. Or maybe, I just wanted a surrogate mother.

I still remember the girls name to this day - Debbie Creasy. Lee Bay Hotel, which is still operating and looks stunning on its own website, dominated the strange bay that surrounded it, with rocky crags and beaches of boulders compared to the usual golden sand. At low tide when one is normally lying making sandcastles and attempting to remove gritty sand out of the crack in your bottom, the view was of a moonscape. No water for hundreds of yards, just rocks, granite, boulders and pebbles. A great place to catch crabs and if Debbie and I had been ten years older, I may have caught them all too easily.

The waves pounded the sea defences at high tide with plumes of salt water crashing over the walls onto the road. 'Oh! Those delightful summer holidays.' It was probably there that I developed a great love of the sea, a frightening, infinite flat land of water, compelling, yet earning total respect in its power, blackness and danger, for those devoid of respect, or unlucky enough to catch it in all its anger.

I was twelve and Debbie was thirteen from London, and spoke in a very strange language that I had not experienced before, and was madly in love with a 14 year old back home. I recall that she was very attractive with a great figure, large breasts and was certainly old for her age. She was thirteen going on sixteen and I was twelve going on nine. The great thing about the hotel was that there was nothing other than the bay within three or four miles and therefore everything in it, and the people who occupied it, once settled in for the night, were fairly captive. The Eagles Hotel California, springs to mind. 'You can check out any time you want, but you can never leave.'

Every other night was always an evening dinner dance where a live band would play the old and modern day classics with ballroom dancing, long dresses comprising 70's floral hues and flowers for the women, and formal dress for the men that could afford it, dress suits for those who couldn't. I remember so vividly, the songs they played to kick off the evening, a foxtrot, a waltz and on occasion a Military Two-step, followed by Chirpy, Chirpy, Cheep, Cheep and Tie a Yellow Ribbon Around The Old Oak Tree. You could also Knock

Three Times on the Ceiling if you Want Me! It all seemed so natural, safe and fun in those days, albeit, a little stuffy and rather formal; 'Some danced to remember, some danced to forget.'

Debbie was as fit as a butcher's dog and confident with it although her cockney accent drove me bonkers. I had never really come into much contact with any other young females other than my sister Pip, to whom I always appeared a major embarrassment, as any younger brother would do four years her junior. My relationship with Debbie developed, well we played badminton and drank lime and lemonade together. I remember asking her if she fancied going with some other new found friends for a midnight dip (well about nine o'clock really). She said she couldn't because it was her time of the month. I had absolutely no idea what she meant by that and still didn't when she said after my quizzing her that she was on her period. What on earth was she talking about? Had she homework to do or did she have special things to do once a month? What a northern bumpkin I must have appeared. As an aside, I know of many women who have used Tampax the whole of their menstruating life and still couldn't swim or ride a bike!

Only on the last night of the holiday did I realise that this first love resided in the room next to mine, whereas later in my teens, this would have been the first question I would have asked. She had promised to give me a kiss to remember the final evening. We were both destined to escape the Bay the following afternoon when we were due to leave for our respective homes. I clearly remember lying on my bed petrified as she came through the bedroom door.

'Do you want a kiss then?' she demanded.

I was mute. I could not speak from fear of what this may entail, particularly knowing that this hussy was well versed in the art of tonsil tennis and probably a few other things as well.

'What's up, you're not scared are you?' she teased in her Southern drawl.

'No it's just that....,' I was completely shitting my pants.

After twenty minutes debating as to whether we should or shouldn't kiss, she grabbed me by the arm and launched her slug of a tongue into my mouth. It felt exceedingly strange for the first time in my life for another tongue to be rooting out pieces of steak from my upper molars which had been festering there for weeks and I certainly couldn't understand what was happening to my stomach. A plethora of larval caterpillars spectacularly metamorphosed into a rabble of butterflies, fighting to ostracise themselves from my being... and what on earth was going on in my trousers. I wasn't in control and I didn't like it, but it was wonderful.

Well following my first kiss, I certainly didn't want to check out at any time, certainly within the next week. Alas, I was to leave. Mirrors were not on the ceiling and pink champagne was not on ice but it was an out of body experience, certainly in the trouser department. We agreed to wake at seven a.m. the next morning for a repeat match and I was hoping that the tennis would extend to a set or two. I suppose the Sheardie inevitable consequence of 'life's a bitch and then you die' occurred, which in turn has dogged me throughout my years. It set the boundaries and benchmark for the disappointments, the missed opportunities and heartbreak for years to come.

I slept in till nine.

However, we spent the whole of the last morning snogging, (she called it necking), on Lee Bay, amongst the boulders. The only other thing I remember was that she ended up with a locked jaw and spent the final hour of our holidays walking around looking like a basking shark amongst a shoal of plankton. At least it shut her up! I cried on the way home, wrote to her once and never heard from her again.

One other interesting fact about the holidays at Lee Bay which totalled three if my memory serves me correctly, involved another family. We were travelling down again the following year and saw a Ford Cortina broken down on the hard shoulder of the M6. The family had disembarked from the vehicle and were standing safely behind the crash barrier waiting for assistance from the fourth emergency service. My sister turned to my dad and stated that she recognised the family from the previous year from the Hotel and we all turned and had to agree with her. Blow me, two hours after we arrived at Lee Bay, so did they. What a coincidence! It was a shame the car did not contain a pretty girl who suffered from lock jaw and looked like a basking shark with large breasts and a tongue that could move as fast as a salamander.

I always seemed to find an older more experienced girl on every holiday we went on. In Bournemouth one year I met two sisters from Sale in Cheshire, literally up the road from where we lived in Cheadle Hulme, (well two buses away via Piccadilly, Manchester and out again!).

One was a year older and the other was a year younger and I have no idea what their names were, notwithstanding, I did at the time I hasten to add. (I just wasn't that type of boy!). Below the hotel was a games room with a juke box and I remember spending loads of money playing my favourite two tunes of mine at that time; 'Don't Go Breaking My Heart,' sung by Elton John and Kiki Dee, and The Isley Brothers, 'Harvest for the World', which I still love.

I remember snogging (amongst other things) with the older sister next to the juke box. I'm not going to go into relationships and naughty sex talk during this book as my mother and wife may take the trouble to read it, however, she did touch my 'Boy Hood'. I was totally shocked and asked her why she had done this.

'You have to do that to keep a lad around our way, else he'll just piss you off and find someone who will,' she replied, matter of factly. I asked my mum and dad later at dinner if we could move to Sale.

A month after we were back from the holiday, I did actually take the four buses in and out of Manchester and back in and out of Manchester to see her again in sunny Sale. I have to say that the Bournemouth air, sun and holiday atmosphere made her appear a little more demure and sexy than drab Sale. I wouldn't say she was ugly but I did keep a picture of her later on in life on the mantelpiece to keep my kids away from the fire.

No doubts therefore why she had to do what she had to do next to the juke box. However, one strange fact that emerged following the telephone call advising her that I couldn't afford the 2p bus fare into town which, when timed by four was 8p, and would not be visiting her again.

Her sister phoned straight after I put the phone down and asked me out. How strange was that! I wouldn't mind but she was far more attractive than her sister, although she probably wouldn't have had to do a 'juke box', to keep a fella. Still, she wasn't worth the bus fare either. 8p is 8p.

I loved those holidays with the family over the teen years, not just for the experience itself, but for the fact that I was hundreds of miles away from the borstal of the school I attended. Everything was so much more simple then. (There is a song in there somewhere). The unrelenting sun baked down, day in day out. The sky, azure blue, and heavenly turquoise seas, reflected the warmth radiating from the star our world orbits, crimson sunsets across the horizon as it slowly turned, warming and embracing other latitudes on our beautiful planet. What a load of rubbish! It always pissed it down!

When I was old enough, it was time to move on and face the world of holidays without parents and siblings and go for it with your mates. It's party time boys!

I went on two holidays with friends met through tennis. One was a disaster and one was brilliant. The first was, believe it or not, a narrow boat holiday on the Cheshire Waterways. At 17, I could not believe that they had allowed us to hire the boat, as five lads full of testosterone were just going to cause chaos and we did not disappoint. I think it has something to do with the fact that one of the lad's fathers worked on the waterways.

We were permanently drunk, falling off the side, nearly crushed a cabin cruiser and were threatened by locals in a number of villages. Any lads out there who are planning such a trip, don't stop in Winsford and take a knife out with you in Audlam. Also, take a girlfriend for something to play with, because it was the most boring holiday you could ever experience as a seventeen year old.

There were a few laughs though. One of the boys, Ronnie fell asleep on his bunk one night. As he lay slumbering in sleep's safe respite, we decided to rearrange his face. Nothing quite as dramatic as had befallen one of the lads the previous night when he had been beaten up in sunny Audlam after calling his attacker's girlfriend a 'complete and utter dog'.

Out came the shaving foam which was duly sprayed over his face, two holes drilled through into his nostrils with a pencil to allow uninhibited breathing. Out came the Sugar Puffs and Cornflakes which were duly shaken onto the cake base. Out came the No 6 cigarettes which were dispatched to form spiky hair akin to Charlie Brown.

He wasn't impressed.

The other holiday was a year later when the same five, (most of which comprised the Tennis Cheshire under 18 Team), went to Ibiza and stayed in San Antonio. It was rocking even then with more bars, clubs and discos per square mile than any other place in Europe. For those who enjoy nostalgia, Dire Straits, 'Sultans of Swing', and Chic's, 'Le Freak', were the top tunes at the time. Any youngsters reading this - You think you know it all! We did it all years ago! We invented the all-nighters and raves, not you lot! Get your own genre, own fashion and your own lives and stop copying all that has gone before you. We were suffocating in buxom breasts and blowing up condoms before you even became spermatozoa.

I remember only a few things about the holiday, as once again, we were constantly pissed for the whole two weeks. We were due to take off from Manchester Airport at 10.00 p.m., however, there were major delays and we did not depart until six in the morning. I remember that we had a pint an hour over those eight hours and nowadays would not even have been allowed on the flight due to our intoxicated bawdiness.

Upon arrival at the Hotel, which I think was at around 11.00 a.m. we went straight out to sunbathe amongst the Germans. Bloody hell, aren't they a big race! I slept all day and woke up at six o'clock in the evening under a large towel, trying to protect myself from the sun's rays. Total, complete and utter 2nd degree burns from the searing heat covered the whole of the front of my once white body. I had never experienced this before but would do on virtually every holiday since. When will I ever learn? Probably never! I thought it would be good to get brown as a berry on the first day. I didn't realise that it took a little longer and one had to be careful in heat hot enough to boil an egg on the blacktop. I really struggled to dance to Chic in the disco that night. The whole of my body was rigid.

Another thing I remember was a very buxom German girl stopped me getting beaten up one night by a bunch of blond giants, straight out of the German Hitler Youth camps. I repaid the compliment in my own way and she seemed rather pleased. I can't speak German but she could speak some English. 'Ya that is gud', is all I remember. I would refuse to ever do this again though. The hairs from her armpits were so long; they were plaited and tied to the top of her tights to hold them up. Still, at least she had shaved her chest. She had huge balls though!!

One night, my pal and I copped off with a couple of girls from Sweden. He went off with blonde Freda and I ended up back at the apartment lying on the bed of the only dark haired, ugly, frigid Swede ever born. She just happened to take a liking to me. 'Oh Good!'

Gurtenburger, I think was her name, stated that she did not kiss young men and promptly stomped off to the bathroom to trim her nose hairs. Just at that moment, her room-mate who was in the bed opposite, called me over. She was an absolutely stunning, blonde Swede that made the girls from Abba look like seal culling fishing vessels. She was the Goddesses, Aphrodite, Artemis, Venus and Diana all wrapped up in one five foot five package.

'Ven you have finished wiv Gurtenburger, you may hav me!' she purred, as she pulled away the sheets to reveal a bronzed body clothed in underwear as small, and unused, as a fine lady's handkerchief.

'I'm really sorry, but I just couldn't! I couldn't be that cruel to your friend.'

'Maybe ve vill meet again sometime. I truly hope so!'

'I hope so too!' I sobbed.

The only place I would ever meet her again would be in Acielus or Poseidon.

The story of my life! What a complete and utter dickhead! At least I can say that I was loyal and faithful to a frigid, ugly, mousey, haired Swede with long nose hair whom I'd known for an hour.

There again honour is honour and I can hold my head up high. Tell you what though! I could have held my head up even higher if I had made the choice of the cad!

Possibly the best chance of my fiery, hormonal, teenage life was missed on that occasion, but I do not regret the decision I made....Like hell I don't!

CHAPTER FOUR:

Back to very dark days

I want somehow to tell the story of how the dispossessed become possessed of their own history without losing sight, without forgetting the meaning or nature of that journey – Sherley Anne Williams

It was the first day of my A-Levels. I had two first papers lasting three hours on the same morning. I therefore had to sit in the Deputy Head's office during lunch in order that I could do the other paper in the afternoon without speaking to anyone. If I recall, it was English Literature in the morning and Sociology in the afternoon. What I didn't realise was the total waste of time it was going to be sitting either but in particular the Sociology first paper. Out of the fifteen people who took the exam, only one person passed with an E grade. Funnily enough, he was the one pupil out of the fifteen taking the course that had joined after the first year. Obviously, the longer you study Sociology, the worse you become at it!

I remember the day was tough graft. 'A' Levels in those days were tough and to pass you actually had to do some work and not just be able to write your name on the top of the paper with the correct date. Flippant, I know but based on statistics, more and more youngsters seem to pass with flying colours without the work involved in the old days. And whilst I'm spouting off, what's all this rubbish about course work contributing to the overall mark. Not only that, but if it isn't good enough, you can do it again and again and again until it *is* good enough. What a load of bollocks! In my day, you had two, three hour exams, and if you didn't pass them you were knackered!

Anyway, on this fateful day in June, the 6th to be precise in 1978, it was a glorious day, summer blossom, fragrant nectar of blooms, heat arising from the asphalt, shimmering like an oasis, each car floating on air down the main road outside Bedlam. I left the school following the final ill-fated exam and caught the bus home. It was just like any other day other than my 'A' levels had started, and I was moving into adulthood.

I had already secured a job as a management trainee with Lewis's Department store in Manchester, however, this was dependant on me obtaining two A level passes. I had also been offered jobs at British Home Stores and Debenhams on their Management Training Programmes and just for good measure, had applied to Midland Bank as a back-up to be offered a job as a trainee.

'It's a job for life lad,' my dad had said a few days before when the offer letter came through. Little did he know that in the future, banking would become an insecure and fairly precarious career. This has arisen mainly due to the greedy fat cats at the top, who are only bothered about the few years they are employed. They want to make an impression, speculate investments to generate immediate profit and arrogantly tender securitisation, selling on or buying debt, with no knowledge of the quality of the lending. Let's be honest, prudence, conservatism and caution were all we were taught in our young banking days. Well didn't they do so in the years up to and including 2008/9?

What my father also didn't know was that he wouldn't have the opportunity of saying many other words in his life time.

That afternoon I returned home, fairly knackered and had tea with mum. Dad was due in from work at Clayton Aniline Company early, as he had a tennis match at Ryecroft Park Tennis Club in the annual singles competition. The whole family played at the club and I was fortunate to win the Men's Singles competition in later years (and lose in a further three!!). I remember him signing up for the tournament and I think I was playing with him in the Men's doubles. 'Go on, stick me down for the singles as well,' he bravely declared. The name was placed on the sheet and the job was a 'gud un'.

I remember him coming in, in his work suit, smelling as always, rather strange, chemicals, dye stuffs who knows, but it was a strange smell, a factory smell but not a smell emanating from a factory producing Hovis Family Loafs or freshly baked baps.

I remember the meal he had had prepared by my mum; salad with a piece of salmon, a light meal prior to his match against one of the regular players on the second team, Peter Walters. Dad set off, and the family who were very well known at the club from a social and playing perspective, pottered down slightly later to enjoy the atmosphere, chat to friends and pals, and watch any matches going on that night. It was a beautiful June evening, and whilst tired from failing my exams both morning and afternoon I was content to enjoy a beer and watch dad thrashing away.

Dad was 51 in the March of that year and was without doubt a little overweight, although he had just lost a stone in weight from a rigorous diet instigated by mother. I was a bit bored as both were steady players and the rallies seem to go on forever. I had passed my driving test and drove mum's white Ford Escort a lot of the time. I decided to go to the nearest off licence to purchase some discount cigarettes. I think they were called 555s but I am not sure. I smoked one and drove back to the club and saw my mum, my sister, Pip, and then husband, Dave, amongst others, sitting on a bench watching dad play against his opponent. The match had gone on and on and on and the heat was obviously starting to affect both players.

I was watching and till this day, am adamant that I had a premonition. It's a bit like when you think of someone, just before the phone rings and it's them on the phone, but not only that but you know as soon as it rings that is them on the phone. I thought to myself, when he has his heart attack do I climb over the fencing surrounding the court, or do I run around the side of the court, turn 90 degrees left, run along the court to the gate, turn left through the gate and then across two courts to him. Anyway, it was a pathetic thought and continued to watch the match to its conclusion where dad lost 7-5 in the third set.

We all clapped and the two shook hands. Dad walked off the court and sat on a small wall adjacent to the court, mopping his brow. Suddenly his head tipped to one side and he dropped down to the shale having suffered a major heart attack.

For those of you who want to know, you sad bastards, I did not go over the netting but around the courts, as people began to congregate around him. I ran up to him and did not have to usher people away, there was no one trying to do anything, as I recall. Dad always has had false teeth from losing half of them wicket keeping as a youngster and having the rest removed as was seemingly the thing to do in the 40's / 50's. I will never forget removing them, both top and bottom and placing both sets on his tennis racket.

I was a 17 year old, innocent, immature child and I was surrounded by at least 20 adults. However, no one attempted to do anything and it was as though we were the only two humans on the planet, my dad and I, one dying, one crying. My sister and brother in law had gone to phone the ambulance, the station for which was literally 500 yards from the club. I started pumping his chest, and breathing down his mouth. I can still remember the smell of salmon emanating from his dying body. I had never been taught CPR and had no clue as to what to do. Regrettably, neither did any of the other 30 players and spectators that had swollen by the minute to come to view the lonely death of my father.

I turned to a chap called Derek Paul. Dr Derek Paul. 'Do something, you're a doctor.'

'I'm not a Doctor of Medicine,' came the reply. I did think to myself at that time, why are you called a Doctor if you aren't a Doctor. What are you a Doctor of – ineptitude? Just in passing, Dr Paul also died in the same situation five years later and his son whom I played on numerous occasions was a complete and utter pillock!

I continued to pump and push and breathe into his mouth and still I was alone. No one took control and I was left to save his life, viewed by a gallery of aged on-lookers, with not one ounce of first aid training between them.

(At this point, may I say if you are planning to have a heart attack, I do not suggest you join Ryecroft Park Tennis Club. 'Oh! someone else has pegged out, is it my serve or yours, Roger?')

I remember looking into his eyes and in my heart I knew he was already dead, lying on the shale. The ambulance took around five minutes to arrive and he, my mum and my sister were taken to Stepping Hill hospital in Stockport. I took the car and drove in order that I could bring them back. We were taken to a room and within a few minutes, a doctor came in to confirm our worst fears.

Losing a parent at any age is a heartbreaking affair and grief manifests itself in many ways. I, other than that evening, really never cried for the loss of my father, which did concern the remaining family somewhat. Of course I loved him deeply. However, did I know him?

It's a strange relationship father and son. Dads normally are inseparable from their daughters whilst most sons, particularly when they are the youngest, are very close to their mothers. Having a nineteen year old son now myself, I really believe that it is only when the son becomes a man and moves into the age of car driving, university and house purchasing, that they really get to know each other. This, I know is a gross generalisation and every relationship is different.

To be honest, I hardly knew my dad, his characteristics, his likes and dislikes and feelings and it is this that I really regret. There is the old saying, 'If you could talk to anyone who is living or dead, who would it be?' I would have to say my father.

I actually took the rest of my exams that fateful week and even though a letter was sent from the school to advise the examining body of the tragic loss, they took no notice. This was probably due to the fact that the first two papers I did on the Monday were so bad I would never have passed anyway.

As my choice of job offers had already been decided, Mum contacted Lewis Department Store in Manchester when I received the awful results in August and told them the circumstances. Very kindly they advised that it was tough shit and as I hadn't passed, I couldn't go on the Trainee Management Programme. I think Lewis's actually went bust a number of years ago. Excellent news!

The only thing I remember of my Dad's funeral was the fact that the hearse we were riding in travelled to Stockport Crematorium at a speed of approximately 18 miles an hour. I pointed out the fact that the speedometer went up to 160 miles an hour. The family riding in the car were almost in tears, laughing uncontrollably. What a very bizarre occurrence, a wife, daughter and son being driven to bury their husband and father, laughing. It is very strange what we find funny and in particular the times we do so.

In the September of that year my mum found out that she had angina. In the October my sister had a double thrombosis, one in her leg and one in her lung. In the December my granddad (Mum's side) died and in the January of 1979 I was prime suspect in a rape case.

No I didn't do it!!!

One of my mum's teaching colleagues lived a few hundred years from our house. On one evening, a young man broke into her house and raped her daughter as she lay asleep in her bed; A truly horrific experience. Because of the connection of the families and the close proximity of the houses, I of course, was on the top of the, 'I think we need to interview this one, Sarge,' list. When they called, I was not in at the time and they actually searched my bedroom for an hour. I have no idea whether they had a search warrant or not and the effect it must have had on my mum is unimaginable.

They called back and interviewed me for around an hour and a half and asked me if required, would I provide a semen sample? No I'm not going to make any jokes whatsoever about policemen's helmets and why are policeman's balls bigger than fireman's, and just to clarify, they did not actually mean they required one at that specific moment. Had they wanted a stool sample, I could have provided it there and then.

Anyway, all things went quiet over the next few weeks, albeit, some of my mates were also interviewed. The sick bastard perpetrator was finally caught and if I, and certainly the family whose lives he had ruined, had any say in his fate, his penis and scrotum would have been removed without anaesthetic.

So all in all, those seven months from June 1978 to January 1979, formed a totally dreadful period in my life. Together with the bullying experiences, I was a quite mixed kind of guy up by the age of 18. In theory, I could have lost the whole of my family in half a year, all from different causes.

CHAPTER FIVE:

Rock and Roll, Clubs and Balls.

Maturity is the capacity to withstand ego-destroying experiences, and not lose one's perspective in the ego-building experiences – Roberts K. Greenleaf

I have purposely not written much in this ramble about my life from 1978 to date. For one thing, I don't think anyone would be remotely interested and secondly, for the vast part, the period has been fairly mundane with the same things appearing to happen, week in, week out. Life just appears to pass by with such speed as you drift through the decades in adult life and it is impossible to comprehend where the time has gone. In Shakespeare's 'The Tempest', Prospero openly talks to his beautiful daughter, Miranda about the fleeting qualities of life. How true this is.

I have only been married once and still remain so, to a beautiful and feisty Italian. Rosa and I are looking forward to our twenty fifth wedding anniversary this year (2009) in August. I have not mentioned the date because I can never remember whether it is the fourth or fifth!

I also have two wonderful, beautiful sons, Daniel who is now nineteen and David who is twelve. Both are massively talented in many ways and in particular, their musical ability. Both can play virtually any instrument that is presented to them and I hope that this pastime continues to be a huge part of their lives for many years to come. They are personable, loving people and I am immensely proud of them. All my family have stood by me, on occasions, in very difficult circumstances, and I truly thank them for their patience and love. Fatherhood didn't start off in the way I had anticipated.

I have to say that childbirth itself is the most frightening experience I have ever witnessed or been a part of. I was traumatised seeing my wife endure such pain and what most would say was the best moment of their lives, I would hasten to add that I did not. This statement will no doubt cause outrage amongst you mothers out there and I, of course, know why you would think that. But to see a loved one go through that is heartrending. There has been so much pressure for men to be present at the birth over the last few decades and it now appears to be the 'done thing' and I believe that some men just have not got the strength on occasion. Whilst I totally empathise with the woman and the suffering they endure, little is given by way of counselling for those that have to witness such agony and ordeal. I was profoundly traumatised by the whole thing and struggled to overcome this in the first few months of their lives.

Anyway back to lighter things! Music has played a huge part in my life too and Rosa and I have played in a band for many years. Whilst the genre of music has changed over the last thirty years the enjoyment has never faltered. Kings Ransom was the original name and Rosa was the singer and I played bass and sang. Along with my estranged brother-in-law Dave on guitar and long standing friend Martin Jones on drums we originally played rock folk. We appeared at a number of festivals across the country and were lucky enough to work with Joe Beard (ex Purple Gang), on the lives and legends of Alderley Edge in words and music. This appeared on Radio Manchester in a one hour special and was broadcast twice.

Throughout the years we played some great gigs and some very unusual ones. We actually played at Styal Women's Prison in Cheshire for the inmates. I know, I know, it was a captive audience. It was also very, very scary. To arrive on a beautiful sunny May day bank holiday afternoon and have to take the cars through a double set of thirty feet high perimeter fencing was an interesting experience. I will never forget us setting up in the empty hall and then the prisoners were escorted in, some with pushchairs, and they all sat around on benches. Rosa and I walked across the room to the back to speak to the warder as to how long we were to play for. As we were strolling, I heard one of the inmates say, 'Fuckin ell! What a lovely arse!' I proudly looked across to see what beauties were mentally undressing me, only to discover that they were looking at Rosa.

We also received a good ticking off that day from the warder. We finished the set at 2.30 p.m. and following a rousing cheer, I shouted the typical muso chant, 'Do you want some more?' This was totally unacceptable to the prison service. Finish at 2.30 p.m. meant you finished at 2.30 p.m..The thought that the in-mates could be allowed an additional 5 minutes was totally unacceptable and with hindsight I totally agree. They had already endured us for an hour and I think that was punishment enough for the day. I am sure they were all desperate to return to their cells.

Another really odd gig we performed was at a motorway service station. Lymm truck stop was an overnight stopping place for lorry drivers and was not open to the general motorist. We arrived and set up. Sitting at fourteen tables were fourteen clones – blue all-in-one overalls, everyone of them completely knackered, nobody talking, everyone alone. What a miserable existence that must be.

We completed the first song which finished with a crescendo, Martin rolling around the toms and finishing with a cymbal crash. Duh, duh, duh, crash. Not a sound. No talking, no clapping, not even a clunk of a pint pot as it was returned to the beer mat. Nothing! It was the most bizarre experience I have ever encountered. Yes, we have had occasion when some dickweed has shouted, 'Get off, you're shite,' to impress his clapping friends, but never to this day have we played where you could hear a pin drop in between the songs. I should have known that it was going to be an odd night. When Dave arrived, he drove into the car park and as he turned and waved to us he launched his Ford Fiesta into the wall of the building. Then Tony who was our second guitar at the time, proudly arrived with his new amplification system that he himself had built.

It was a massive affair with a huge tweeter cabinet on top of a huger mid-range cabinet, on top of an even huger base cabinet. On top of the lot was an amp head. The stack was approximately eight feet high and would have looked perfect on the main stage at Knebworth. I have to say it did look at little out of place on the main stage at Lymm Truck Stop.

He proudly set this up and plugged all the constituent parts together. Unfortunately, he inadvertently touched a guitar string with the effects jack plug and it immediately exploded the string with a puff of blue smoke rising into the air. Not believing that his giant rig was not earthed, he did it again to see whether it would have the same effect. It did. When he finally managed to replace the strings which had melted with new ones, he managed to plug in without killing himself and cranked up the stack. It sounded shite. What a strange night that was.

We played countless gigs all over the North West of England and even travelled up to Tarbert in Scotland to attend a music festival in the harbour. I'll never forget the lone piper standing at the front of a small motor boat piping the commencement of the festivities. It was a haunting sight indeed with a rolling cotton mist swirling past his tartan skirts and the drone of the pipe drifting across the bay. People had travelled from all over Scotland to the event and it coincided with a Tall Ships Race leg.

These stunning boats had moored in the harbour overnight prior to their next leg of the race and their occupants contributed to a strange array of people in the town that night. They ranged from the blue jacketed, gold button, white pump, upper class brigade to yobbos from Glasgow who had made the pilgrimage to this dreamy fishing port to attempt to drink it dry.

We had kindly been lent Rosa's school minibus to take us and the equipment up for the weekend. Adorning the side of the blue bus were the words 'St Thomas's Roman Catholic High School' emblazoned in large white lettering. It is amazing that in the company of the jocks and the fact that there wasn't a Catholic church within one hundred miles, the aforementioned was not torched and up ended. To the contrary, one drunken nutter asked if he could use the toilet and another walked up whilst we were sitting in between gigs, and asked for one cheeseburger and three portions of chips.

I thought I drank and swore a lot. I am a mere novice in this respect. The gigs were undoubtedly scary and I was pleased that we all left in one piece particularly following the final gig when we stupidly played an Oyster Band song entitled The Rose of England promptly followed by Hard Times of Old England by Steeleye Span. What bravery in the face of the Tartan Army.

We probably reached the height of our musical career in this phase and played many festivals including Fylde and Redcar and regularly performed in front of 500 to 1000 folk fans in sizeable venues, treading the boards with Big Country. However, the music style drifted away from folk. We were too folky for rockers and too rocky for folkies. You could see the traditionalists in the audience, pewter tankards attached to their belts, with fingers in their ears and it wasn't so they could pitch a harmony. We also had a fairly large P.A. set up and we were just too big, size wise, to play many small clubs. We turned to country rock and then blues, in many respects, playing to the strengths of the personnel which made up the band at any one time. We also dropped the 'Kings' and the band is still known to this day as 'Ransom'. We hosted a singers night at Didsbury Cricket Club for 22 years, however, following the demise of live music connoisseurs, ended up playing in front of the bar lady and the club cat on numerous occasions and we finally gave it up.

One story which could have been placed in numerous sections of this book, for example, 'most embarrassing moments', or 'Murphy's Law', concerned one of our drummers who will remain nameless. He had recently split up from his wife and was on the lookout for a new soul mate.

Whilst working on his house, he had said hello to a lady who used to walk her dog down the street on a regular basis. After selling the matrimonial abode, he thought nothing of his regular acknowledgement until one day he received a text message.

The woman in question had seen his number on the side of his van and written it down prior to him leaving the area and had texted him initially to say hello. Texts were exchanged and they became more and more fruity until, finally, they decided to meet.

They arranged to get together in one of the most romantic places on earth, stuff of dreams.... in a B&Q car park.

Following a full and frank discussion where it was revealed that whilst the woman was married, she fancied embarking on a 'strings free sexual relationship'.

'Lucky bastard,' I would say!

They tonsil tennised for about half an hour in her car until the windows steamed up and it was attracting attention from the general public. People were streaming out of the store, clutching Polyfilla, 2" by 2", and light fittings, only to be confronted by a Citroen Saxo masquerading as a mobile sauna. In addition, fifteen teenagers had decided to stage an FA Cup knock out match in the car park and the car with steamy windows formed an ideal goal. Our friend's new love decided to move the car into the corner of the expansive park to continue the licking sessions.

With a tongue as stretched as a desert lizard in a sandstorm, she finally confessed that she would have to return to her uninformed husband. Grudgingly our intrepid Ginger Baker opened the van door and walked across the car park to his van. Flicking the electronic alarm, he unlocked the doors, opened the driver's door and rolled in. Starting up the engine, he pulled away, driving the length of the car park to wave at his new found playmate.

He followed in his van to the end of the entrance road and turned the opposite way, flashing his lights in a final act of affection to drive home, happy in the knowledge that he could indulge in sexual gratification at the press of a button for the foreseeable future.

He drove twelve of the fourteen miles home and noticed that the car was running short of diesel. Pulling into an Esso filling station, he filled the tank and searched for his phone and wallet to pay. The wallet was on the passenger seat however he was unable to find his phone. He went and paid for the petrol and returned to the van.

He pulled into the gas and air bay and continued the search. Suddenly he went white with fear and a cold sweat dissipated a bead at the nape of his neck. The phone had been in his pocket when he had boarded her car and must have dropped out into her car when he was frolicking.

'Oh! My God!'

Turning out of the petrol station, he raced down the road and back onto the motorway. Panic gripped our loveable beat box as he screamed through each gear, blasting the air with diesel fumes as the van raced through the darkening night.

The only problem was, he didn't know exactly where she lived, only roughly. Arriving at the locality of where he thought she may reside, he commenced curb crawling the streets looking for any sign of her car. He even became so desperate that he started scanning the pavements for dog faeces left by her whilst walking. (Well not by her but by the other end of the leash.)

He finally recognised her car, not from the make and model but from the unnatural amount of surface water on the windows. But what should he do? He could not text or telephone her and if her husband found his phone in her car and read the text messages..... Well it did not bear thinking about. The only thing for it was to knock on the door.

He alighted the van and walked up to the curtained semi-detached and rang the bell, a concocted story requesting directions poised on his war weary tongue, should the male of the house answer the door. Heart pounding, beads of sweat caressing the crack of his builder's bottom, the door slowly opened. Thank God it was his floosie.

'What the hell are you doing here?' she spurted, pushing him away from the door, 'My husband is in!'

'I've left my phone in your car, I must have dropped it!'

'I'll look for it but just go, for God's sake, he will kill you!'

'Tell him I was seeking directions to the local sports centre,' be blurted.

The rhythm master turned and went back to his van which was parked at the end of her drive. He quickly entered, turned the key and placed the vehicle into gear.

Rather than speed off forwards, the van shot back. Now whilst this story could have concluded that the van reversed into her husband's car, it did not. It merely went backwards hugging the curb. Our hero realised his mistake and was just about to change back to first, he noticed that his girlfriend's lounge curtains had been parted – not the first thing that night that had been parted - and was owned by his girlfriend.

His amour's husband was peering out of the window as the van rolled backwards. Rather that engage first gear, our suitor continued his passage in reverse, smiled, raised a hand and waved to the husband.

The husband waved back!

Our drummer then proceeded to realise that he was reversing further into the cul-de-sac and there was no way out. He therefore placed the van into first and accelerated away. The curtain was still open with the man staring out into the night. Once again my pal smiled and waved at the beleaguered husband.

Once again the husband waved back.

The drummer combed his hair with his fingers as he sped away and dropped his hand to the centre console panel straight onto his mobile phone which had been there stored safely, for the whole of the evening.

What a numpty. But what a great guy also.

Nothing in this world can give you such a buzz as to play in a band, go down really well and the crowd yell for more. It is a part of my life which has been so special, and whilst we are doing less and less every year I still enjoy making music. In the cellars at our house I have a small studio and I am concentrating on writing a lot more of my own compositions and feel that this will be the way forward as I drift into old age. My dream is to write a solo album, playing all the instruments myself and also to write a rock musical. Who knows!

Sports have been fairly prevalent in my enjoyment of life, turning from tennis to golf in my thirties. Both of these sports have given hours and hours of pleasure. Amazingly, I manage to play off a twelve handicap at golf and truly have the worst swing in the club. I always advocate that it is where the ball ends up and not how it gets there that is important. That is my excuse anyway.

I was once at the club (Bramhall G.C.) standing near the club house adjacent to the first tee when a man came running from the course. He was panting heavily and was very much in a state of panic. 'Quick, quick,' he shouted. 'The lady Captain has been hit by a stray golf ball.'

'That's terrible,' I replied. 'Where has she been hit?'

'In between the first and second holes,' came the response.

'Where are they going to put the plaster?' I retorted.

The golf course has provided some memorable moments and great jokes and I have thoroughly enjoyed the crack with a fantastic mate, Andy Pennie. We are the Laurel and Hardy of the golf club, known for our cordial and relaxed company and our odd appearance, with Andy towering to six foot three against my five foot eight. But my God we have had some laughs.

'When there is a storm cloud and lightning is spiking down onto the course do you hide under a tree or away from the trees, George?'

'I walk down the centre of the fairway with a one iron in my hand pointing it up to the Gods, Crispin.'

'Why do you do that George?'

'Because even God can not hit a one iron.'

I had the honour of having to attend a dinner with my golf partner of ten years following a win in some competition. He drew the short straw and had to present the acceptance speech. We always have an argument as to who is going to do this and we normally say that it is the player who played worse during the round. Andy is brilliant at speeches and I was totally happy that he would be undertaking this scary task. It contained the following joke.

A man was playing golf with some friends one day and he sliced his ball into the rough. When he approached the misdirected projectile, it was sitting on a buttercup. Not minding that he was breaking a rule of golf as this was a friendly match, he picked up the ball and moved it six inches away from the flower, chose a club and hit the ball onto the green.

Suddenly out of the bushes a small elf appeared. The man was transfixed and stunned at the apparition and could not move. The elf ambled up to the golfer and said in a small gentle voice,

'Why did you move your ball, Sir?'

'I love nature and I wanted to protect that beautiful little flower from the club head, for it would wither and die and no longer bless our beautiful planet,' stuttered the golfer.

'Your love of nature is undoubted and for your thoughtfulness saving the buttercup, you will have as much butter as you can eat for the rest of your life,' said the elf.

'Where the hell were you last week when I moved my ball off the pussy-willow?' said the golfer.

The final one I will tell (I could go on all night) related to an old timer, Cuthbert, who was renowned for being the most miserable, grumpiest and rudest golfer on the planet. He was playing golf with three of the other members of the club and all were walking down the fifteenth hole, which ran parallel to a road. As they walked, they noticed a funeral cortege moving slowly down the lane towards them. As the hearse drew nearer, Cuthbert took off his cap, bowed his head and closed his eyes in solemn reflection. The vehicles passed, Cuthbert re-donned his hat and set off again to find his ball.

'Cuthbert, that was a respectful thing for you to have done, I'm very impressed!' exclaimed his partner.

'Well I was married to her for thirty seven years,' replied Cuthbert.

CHAPTER SIX:

Working Life

All our resolves and decisions are made in a mood or frame of mind which is certain to change – Marcel Proust

Two great human institutions were apparently augurated together, proprietary marriage and the division of society into masters and servants – Emily James Putnam

I've been in banking my entire working career, all 30 years of it and I have to say that my inaction in finding employment which I could have enjoyed more, especially when I was younger, depresses me greatly. Yes, there have been some great times and I've made some very good friends but my heart has always lain elsewhere. Whilst I thoroughly enjoy my present role I would have loved to have spent my working life in the arts and especially in the music industry and I really envy those who can follow a vocation. When I joined the bank in October 1978, I like many people who have done similar, just fell into the industry, rather than longed to do it.

How many teenagers do you meet who say that they are longing to join a high street bank and have done so since they were four?

The work and in particular, the formality has changed beyond recognition over the years, mostly due to advances in technology and the shift towards a sales related environment. Even in the seventies, as a junior, you called the bank manager, 'Mister', and he often called you by your surname. All processing was done in the back office and was a very manual affair. Branches which used to house 30-35 staff in the seventies, now employ anything between 4 and 6 staff, as processing shifted into processing centres to reduce cost. Footfall in the banking halls has fallen dramatically due to cash machines and internet banking.

As I said, some of the people I have met have been brilliant friends and characters abound in the industry. Also some of the stories over the years are somewhat amusing.

I've worked at many branches all of which are domiciled in the 20 mile radius of my home, and presently hold the position of a commercial manager looking after 120 small to medium sized businesses with turnover up to £25 million. I started at Cheadle branch on the 9th October 1978 and the work was very labour intensive, more like a paper production line, where everything had to balance and be checked on a daily or weekly basis. This even included the paying in books which were filed behind cards, a card being designated to every customer of the branch. In those times, if anything didn't balance, you didn't go home and overtime payments formed the staple diet of the monthly pay cheque. My starting salary was £1,722 per annum.

Once you had graduated in cheque processing and other

mundane tasks such as taking postal orders to the Post Office every day, you were promoted onto the counter. I tell you what though, I can still count a wodge of money bloody quickly, not that I ever have any money to count these days. Some great stories originated from the counter.

I had a mate at Sale branch who often accompanied me to the sub-branch in Ashton-on-Mersey, a small two hander where we just ate crisps and read the newspapers all day. If a customer came in, it was really busy. If the customer brought her dog in, it was chaos and sometimes you could count on one hand the number of clients you served in any one day.

Nearly all of the bank branches in those times were very old fashioned with the glass counter area accessible by a lockable door. Behind the counter was always a high wooden wall, tall enough for the back office workers to be able to see what was going on, but not low enough to vault to steal money out of your mate's till. John used to play practical jokes all the time, not just only on the staff but also on customers. One old chap used to come in once a week on a Thursday after picking up his pension from the Post Office. His sole purpose was to change a £5 note into 50p pieces to feed his electricity meter. The counter at the sub office was approximately ten feet wide and his till was at one end with another two stations which were never used. He used to tell the chap that he had to go down into the cellar to obtain the change he required. The coins were of course in his till.

He always did the same thing. He would take £5 of 50ps

from the till without the customer seeing him and then turned to his right and walked along the counter going lower and lower with every step, thus giving the effect that he was going down stairs. By the time he was at the other end of the counter he was on his knees below the level of the counter and out of sight of the customer. He would stay there for a minute crying with laughter and repeated the process in the opposite direction.

On another occasion at the main branch in Sale which had a similar counter, he and another colleague decided it would be really funny one day when the banking hall was empty to put their hands up in the air, as though some charlatan was pointing a gun in their faces. This fell foul when the branch manager came out of his office and saw the four arms aloft and presumed his branch was being raided. Crouching down behind the wooden counter backdrop he crept into the main office on his hands and knees and opened the drawer to obtain a policeman's truncheon and police whistle which was to be used in such an event. Certainly not like the modern day version which would involve the Police Armed Response Unit. I have to say that they did receive a significant rollocking for the prank and I was really not surprised.

There were two other older characters at Sale branch, which also housed the most archetypal, traditional bank manager you could ever meet. Captain Mannering was fun, gregarious and full of spirit compared to this man. Peter and Alan were the characters' names and I remember one day, both went up the stairs to the top floor. They walked down the corridor together, Alan turning right into the gentlemen's toilet and Peter continued to the far end into the kitchen. Peter filled the kettle and switched it on and took out a cup and placed coffee and sugar intending to make a drink.

He then left the kitchen and walked into the gents. One cubical door was locked and Alan was obviously enjoying a good dump. Unfortunately, the aroma from the offending stool steamed from between Alan's bare legs as he sat reflecting and was one of the foulest smells ever to be emitted from a human being.

'You dirty smelly bastard. That is the rankest crap I have ever had the misfortune to snort.'

He decided that he could not stand it long enough to even use the urinal and returned to the kitchen. Alan was standing in the kitchen pouring the hot water into two cups.

'I thought you were in the bog,' he spluttered in the dawning horror of his mistake.

'No, I just went into blow my nose and then went in the stationery room.'

A very red faced and cross bank manager soon exited the room of toxic waste and asked Peter to accompany him to his office for a 'chat'.

Every week in those days, a cash van would visit the branch to either collect or deliver cash and was manned by a senior bank officer and some ordinary staff who were called 'guards'. There were two of these vans, one for notes and one for coin and whenever the coin van called, any juniors had to go outside and carry the bags from the van into the bank. Usually the coin was not in the little plastic bags that you get them in and a bag of say, £250 in 50p pieces, were all loose. It was something for us to do in the branch, yet another mundane task counting £10 of 50ps into each plastic bag. These canvas bags of coin were called shot coin for some strange reason.

I once grabbed two bags of £250 of shot 50ps in both hands i.e. £1,000 in total. However, one of the bags was not tied properly and I dropped it. The branch was on a busy main road and approximately three quarters of the contents spilled out over the pavement all over the road.

We had to stop the traffic in both directions for at least 10 minutes to collect up any that had not either found a grid to fall in, or a passer by's pocket to fall in. I was bollocked by the manager, the officer in charge of the coin van and approximately 76 car and van drivers. We only lost about £4.50 however, and I suppose you could almost call that a result.

I believe ultimately, maybe in ten or fifteen years from now, there will be no counter services at any bank branch, following the recent introduction of new paying in machines and the extension of the ATM network. When all said and done, the cashier and the service that is provided by them is outrageously expensive, when the work could be done, in effect, by the customer themselves, utilising machinery.

The growing number of customers who utilise internet banking appears to grow each and every year and this particular method of banking also takes away the need for staff.

The face of banking is changing rapidly and there are very real prospects for significant job losses through cost cutting, amalgamation and reduction of duplication on the high street. Only recently, Lloyds TBS Group announced that they were closing Cheltenham and Gloucester and is only a matter of time before many household names disappear from our towns and villages.

It is a real shame, however, times change, albeit, not always for the better. Bring back Captain Mannering I say.

My wife, Rosa, used to be a P.E. teacher, a job that I could never do. Whether it is because of the experiences at school or the inability of most teenage children to wipe their own noses, I do not know.

There was a cracking story concerning one of Rosa's ex flat-mates who was working in a special school at the time. The school was there for children who had been excluded from mainstream schools, or had severe learning difficulties and had a very high teacher / pupil ratio.

The lady in question was called Chris, short for Christine and was as tough as they come. She had taken fourteen pupils with another teacher on a day trip and was returning back to Stockport. Her remit was to drop certain children off at school and continue with another three, dropping them off at their homes. She normally was not prepared to do this, however, the children lived on her route home.

Tyrone was the final child on the mini-bus and had decided to not waste time asking to stop for a toilet break and proceeded to excrete a log in his underpants. Battling against the resulting gagging reflex she asked Tyrone where he lived.

'A don't know!' came the response.

'What do you mean, you don't know?'

'A don't know where a live.'

'Why don't you know where you live?' heaved Chris, as the waft of cool air induced by the open window re-circulated the smell of old chicken nuggets and chips.

'A moved a few weeks ago.'

'Well what is your house near, any shops? You know any landmarks?'

'Morrisons.'

Chris turned the mini-bus around and headed for the local Morrisons. As she drove, she wondered why she had ever entered into the world of teaching. She also consider the possibility of phoning the secretary at the school to find out Tyrone's address but realised that it was gone 5.30 p.m., and the only person in the school would be the cleaner.

She soon arrived at Morrisons and over the next three quarters of an hour, proceeded to comb the area. Back and forth, forth and back she drove, row upon row of terraced houses all exactly the same bar the colour of the curtains. On and on went the purgatory. The smell of the fulsome underpants permeated the fabric of the fourteen seater, ensuring that any occupants for the next three weeks would catch a whiff of the turtles head.

'Why, why, why, why am I doing this? I hate it. I really hate it. I really, really, really hate it!'

Suddenly a scream, rather than a bowel movement, emitted from the back of the bus.

'There, there, there's me mum!'

'Thank Christ for that!' she thought, as she drew up alongside the trawler of a woman in the Nike suit and Reeboks trudging down the road, Morrisons bag containing eight cans of super strength lager in one hand and a lighted roll up in the other.

'Thank Goodness. Mrs Smith, I'm just returning Tyrone home after the school trip. Hop in and I'll give you a lift too.'

'Thank God!' she exclaimed. 'I can't remember where my new house is!'

Maybe I am lucky to work in a bank where the customers nearly always know where they live and most often have control of their bodily functions!

Having said that, one of the members of my current band was a librarian. There was a number of incidents where the police were called to the library he was working in to investigate. Apparently someone kept pooing inside the books, and placed them back on the shelf.

My friend assures me that it wasn't him, although the culprit has never been caught!!!!!

CHAPTER SEVEN:

Simon's stories and more

To live in dialogue with another is to live twice. Joys are doubled by exchange and burdens are cut in half - Wishart

I have changed the name of the following friend and colleague to protect his identity.

I met Simon a number of times prior to working with him. He was what is called in the trade, a 'Financial Planning Manager', an 'FPM' to be brief. FPMs will tell you they do a vital job in protecting businesses and their proprietors against illness, sickness and death.

'Well Mr Jagosinski, how would you feel if you suddenly dropped down dead and what would your fellow directors say.'

'Nothing and thank God!'

These harbingers of doom are the bank's gaggle of grim reapers, selling their wares on the back of the fear of misfortune. Unsurprisingly they have products and services to cover the eventuality of surviving an earthquake or regular plane crash. A pension on the other hand will give you comfort that should you live that long (which is highly unlikely), it will dullen the misery of being a disabled wrinkled old nearly dead, with the comfort of an extra 50p in your purse.

That's a very cynical view and I write it in poetic licence. The service that these colleagues provide, do give significant comfort and protection to our customers and I would encourage all to look after their families and businesses by subscribing to life assurance and pension planning. If you do wish to subscribe, have a word with me and I will sort it for you!!! In addition many of these guys and gals have been great, fun people; none more so than Simon.

If the synopsis were correct, one would expect Simon to be seven foot tall wearing a black hooded cloak, ethereal mist emanating out of the pockets and openings. However, far from this bleak and black vision of destiny stood a five foot five inch bearded gentle man. I was going to describe him akin to Gimley in the Lord of the Rings, however, this would not be the case. Simon was as gentle as they came and very slightly taller.

When I first met him, his career had crossed many paths, some of which were not shared with the likes of me. However, I was aware that he had worked for a paper manufacturer and another high street bank prior to his employ with my bank.

Simon was a kind man, a real twinkle in his eye and always looking for anything to make him laugh. He was a great storyteller, not really a joker per se. One thing that you certainly would realise immediately upon meeting the man was his inordinate ability to talk the hind legs off a donkey. Every donkey I have ever met that Simon had talked to, dragged a small-wheeled cart behind it resting its weary stumps. However it did so with a huge grin, protruding teeth like tombstones, polished with Macleans toothpaste.

A joke was not a joke. It was a tale. It lasted forever and there was no real punch line. When in the mood, happy to while away the day, in a car driving miles to another nearly dead, it was a joy. I once never spoke a word from just outside Congleton in Cheshire to just north of East Sheen but I tell you what - Simon did. When in a hurry, desperate to leave the office to visit a customer and you were late, Simon was a nightmare. Word has it that at least six customers died waiting for the end of Simon's presentations - or was it that they had qualified for their pension before they had signed up for one? One of my colleagues once said that Simon could put a glass eye to sleep.

Nevertheless, Simon's stories were brilliant, and throughout this epitaph, I have attempted to re-tell a number of them. I was going to tell them as Simon had told me, however the publishers decided that they would have to bring volumes out, akin to Encyclopaedia Britannica, in monthly instalments, the first of which would be half price with a free pack of Simon trading cards.

So let me set the scene of this first epic emanating from Simon's period of employment with his previous bank. Simon, as previously mentioned, was a humble man, who wanted to do what was right and best for the customer. His patch in those days was deepest, darkest Salford, not the most affluent or salubrious place in

Manchester to say the least. With its painted matchstick men with clogs, uninitiated ones amongst you would have thought 'How quaint'. Unfortunately, Mr Lowry lived in another century, certainly to the one in which Simon worked. Having said that, Simon in clogs would certainly be a sight for sore eyes and with his groomed beard, would not be out of place in a morris men troupe. Think of that in Salford! I think not!

Regrettably, Salford is grey, damp and foreboding, similar to many inner city early nineteenth century conurbations. As an aside, it is great to see that significant money has been poured into the area to regenerate this urban sprawl in recent years. As such, I am probably doing the place a disservice in the present day, however not 20 years ago when Simon clip clopped his way along the cobbles in his clogs.

Simon was working for another bank in the same role as he subsequently did for my bank. He had had a call from one of the clerks to say that a customer and his wife were very interested in talking to him about pensions and could he call that day to make an appointment. Simon embarked on the telephone call that lunchtime following a snack on BLT on brown, a small cream cake and a Twix (both fingers). The attempted call total was four, having abandoned the previous three, twice to remove food from his beard (lettuce and toffee) and once when he noticed his trouser leg was tucked into his shoe.

The wire finally connected. Alexander Graham Bell could rest again in the knowledge that his amazing invention was helping connect people, devoid of embarrassing tuck ins and foodstuffs.

Anyway, Simon introduced himself to Mr Donaldson stating that his colleague had advised him that Mr and Mrs D might wish to discuss with him issues of a 'nearly dead nature', sorry pensions.

(May I just point out that this is poetic licence and I have every faith in UK pension planning generally. I am allowed to do this because this is my book and if you don't like it, don't bloody read it.)

Mr Donaldson stated that he would like to meet with the miniature Hagred and would he come around the next evening to his humble abode in Salford. Simon duly agreed.

The next evening was a wet one, by God it was; the type that has you ringing out your knickers. Simon felt fairly downbeat as he turned onto the Mancunian way, westwards out of the city. It was autumn and bitterly cold. Leaves and litter flew past in tandem down the street. He stopped at traffic lights swaying in the wind, old newspapers, plastic drink bottles, cigarette packets cleaned the gutters as they swept by. One container thrown up by the mistral caught temporarily under the windscreen wiper – a McDonalds, Strawberry McFlurry box. Roy drove away faintly touching his lips with his tongue, humming 'I'm lovin it!!'

No! He wasn't! Acid arose in his stomach and Simon reached inside a small pocket in his waist coat – I know,

I know but he was a traditional kind of dude – retrieving an antacid. Simon drove on, cursing his luck, finally arriving at the Donaldsons.

The house was sited on a typical inner city street built in the early 1900s to house workers in the mills and factories springing up all over the North of England. Line after line of small terraced houses resembled grid lines from the sky. This was pie, black peas, flat caps and 'E by gum' country tha knows. You Southern jessies have never lived! Traditional two up two downs offered a front room for best, and a back parlour which housed the tiny kitchen, with two small bedrooms upstairs. Bathing was often done in a tin bath in front of the fire and toilet visits comprised a cold trudge to the water closet in the back yard.

Simon alighted his Ford Mondeo, the standard company car of its day, and walked warily up to the front door at which, he rattled the knocker. A few moments later he heard footsteps descending the stairs and the paint-less door opened.

Mr Donaldson was in his early forties with a face that had experienced hundreds of years of wear. I wouldn't say he was ugly but his wife when he was going out used to say, 'Whosyas goin to scare tonite?' This was a true working man, proud, strong and Northern!

'Mr Donaldson, its Simon from the Bank. I spoke to you earlier on the phone.'

'Oh Yes! Come in cock,' replied the pit bull, opening

the door to allow entry. However, Mr D did not allow passage immediately and leaned out half into the street. 'What a bleedin' awful night. Find it alright?'

Simon turned towards the street and confirmed in the affirmative stating that he knew the area and had visited the street before.

Donaldson turned and allowed entry and ushered hapless Simon into the front room, reserved for best. Simon, making his way into the room struggled to take his raincoat off and ended up taking one arm of his jacket off at the same time as both arms of his coat, dislodging pens, business cards and a number of coins onto the threadbare carpet. He glanced back at Mr D in embarrassment. However, he did not seem to be there. Confidently, Simon stepped forward, bending to retrieve the errant articles, however, the toe of his shoe caught on the loose jacket sleeve and a large ripping sound emanated from the unruly apparel.

Simon quickly wrestled off both garments and picked up the items, stuffing them into any pocket he could find and calmly placed the large bundle of pinstripe rags onto a small wooden chair.

Walking to the doorway, Simon popped his head around to see where Mr D was hidden and realised that he had returned to the front door and was looking out again at the wretched evening as though memorised by the elements, or fearful of them.

'Mr Donaldson?'

'Oh sorry! I love the weather. It reminds me of my Gran.'

Both men walked into the front room passing the rolled up remnants of Simon's wardrobe and sat down, Mr D in his, and only his, armchair, and Simon on the furthest end of a two-seat sofa, near the fire.

Simon commenced his sales pitch, extolling the virtues of pension planning and being prudent enough to save for the future. Only two minutes into his soliloquy a medium sized dog came out of the hall and into the room. Simon for once fell mute, and both men turned towards the new entrant as he approached. The dog was a mutt of the highest order, wiry hair matted to itself and a face that had launched a thousand shits.

(It reminds me of a few girls I used to know!)

The dog paused for a moment to contemplate its audience and slowly padded up to the sofa. The half naked banker realised that the dog was about to jump on the other end of the couch and lifted his jotter pad with lined paper off the seat to accommodate. However, the dog rather than jump up, lowered its head and sniffed years of life grime ingrained in the sofa arm. Both men watched transfixed as the dog lifted his head, shuffled forward and lifted its right hind leg. It proceeded to piss the whole content of his dog water bowl over the couch end. His body shook very slightly as it forced out the last remaining drop, licked its lips, moved forward towards the fire, climbed up on the slightly raised hearth, yawned and curled up into foetal position, closing its eyes and went to sleep.

No sound was uttered and the two men stared at each other for a passing second. Simon was unaware as to whether this was a regular routine and the sofa arm was an adopted Salford tree stump, allowing the dog to avoid braving the elements. With fortitude, Simon continued.

'Saving £50 per month into a pension, the government will give a tax rebate resulting in £62.50 per month going in to the plan. How does that sound?'

The deal was brokered, the customer happy in the knowledge that he would receive an additional £36.47 per week to supplement his old age pension at the age of 65 and Simon in the knowledge that he has earned £127.06 commission from the deal.

Exchanging pleasantries, Simon dismantled his coat from his jacket, turned three of the arms outside in, and dressed for the elements, picking up his jotter pad with the lined paper. Shaking Mr Donaldson's hand he stated that it had been a pleasure doing business and headed for the hallway turning left towards the front door and the impending monsoon.

'Just before you go, Simon, I really think the pension idea is good,' offered Mr Donaldson. 'Is there any chance you could come back next week to see my wife, Edna, as she should sign up for one too.'

Mr Donaldson continued. 'Just one thing, Simon, next

time you come, will you not bring your dog!'

This story typifies Simon's luck. If it happened to anyone it had happened to Simon who should have had the smallest bottom on earth for the number of dogs that had come up behind him and taken a chunk out of it.

A very similar occurrence blighted Simon on another excursion into the depths of darkest Manchester. This time he was visiting a couple and once again involved a dog.

The property was slightly bigger this time, a three bed semi with two reception rooms split with two wooden sliding doors. Simon was there to discuss life assurance and he rang the doorbell in his inimitable way, just slightly pressing it, hoping that the bell might not ring and he could go home, poorer but safe.

The bell responded to the touch and cascaded an extract from Beethoven's Ode to Joy in majestic monotone to announce the arrival of the Prince of Pensions. 'Mr Smith, do come in. and thank you for coming,' stated the occupant. Simon rose the final tread of the steps and walked into the hall immediately to be mounted on the leg by a small Heinz 57 variety dog, the size of a large rodent.

'Tess, leave Mr Smith's leg alone.' implored the owner, to no avail. Simon walked with one leg towards the lounge, dragging the other leg as though it had a three foot long wooden splint attached to it. Simon wished that it had had been. Alas! It was Tess, haunches stooped to allow purchase and eyes glazed with passion for his pinstripe.

The occupant and his wife sat down in the two chairs facing the sofa and Simon fell backwards into it, one leg cocked and the other being cocked.

'Tess, leave Mr S's leg alone. Oh, he is so naughty,' stated the woman as she stooped down and grabbed the frustrated canine away from the insurance man. From six inches from the floor, she tossed the dog away towards the hall and fell back into her chair. The dog turned 180 degrees in mid air and launched itself back at the trousered calf, immediately gathering in the excess cloth and proceeded to hammer away once again with impressive fortitude.

'Tess, get off him!' shouted the woman, leaning forward again, this time grabbing the mutt and throwing him from a number of feet towards the door. Exactly the same thing happened and tempers finally snapped. The woman grabbed the dog, slid back one of the wooden sliding doors and launched him into the dining room quickly sliding the door back to the middle. The sex beast stood there panting in solitary confinement.

Simon commenced his sales pitch and handed the couple his card and all the usual FSA regulated documents advising what he could and couldn't do. He started to take down the particulars of the couple when a strange noise emanated out of the dining room. A slow thud sounded and the right hand door of the sliders shook slightly. Simon continued his pitch but the noise took on a regular, rhythmic beat and the door started to shake as if caught in a minor earthquake. Simon continued, the couple looking interested, and appeared totally un-phased by the cacophony of drum beats from the next door room.

Bang, bang, bang, bang, the noise grew louder and louder, the door starting to shake uncontrollably, its edges embracing the casing around it. Bang, bang, bang, bang, bang. The noise was deafening and Simon and the couple were shouting to be heard. The right door suddenly broke away from the lower runner momentarily entering the lounge by a foot only to swing back with a crash causing the right door to partially slide open to around four inches. The sight in the gap captivated Simon's attention.

Staring out of the dining room, on the floor, was a large snake's head, its long red forked tongue protruding with the ensuing agony. The snake was green and purple in colour and scales of soft fur. On the back of the snake, Tess was purchased, rogering seven bells out of its back. A smile formed on the dog's face as the final hip blows found their mark and with the ecstasy of the final thrust, silence deafened the house. If it couldn't shag Roy's leg it would have to impregnate the draught excluder.

I've no idea whether the policy was sold and I suppose it doesn't really matter, but the scenario again emphasises Simon's bad luck and the rule of Murphy's Law. If something bad could happen, it will.

It also reminds me of another story I heard once on the golf course. I was playing with a real card, a rough diamond who had worked his way up from nothing to owning one of the largest manufacturers of double glazed windows in the country at the time, manufacturing 2,000 windows per week. He too had lived in the back streets of a similar district of Manchester and had had a poor, uncompromising upbringing.

He still lived with his parents in a two up two down in a row of terraced houses until his mid twenties, not being able to afford to move out of the bosom of his mother's maternal nest. The family was desperately poor and did not enjoy the experiences, and even basic comforts that every person in Britain should enjoy.

When he was seventeen he regularly got drunk, so inebriated that on many occasions, he did not know where he was or what time of day it was. He was a typical lad with a wicked sense of humour, which stayed with him even in the most drunken of states.

One evening he visited the local hostelry. Having attempted to empty the whole of a firkin barrel into his gullet, he stumbled home, knowing that he was in deep trouble with his mother upon his return, due to his intoxication. Rather than walking down the street where he would be recognised by neighbours and the police alike, he meandered his way home via the alleys behind the rows of terraces. One foot forward two steps back, one foot sideways, one foot forward, three steps forward, one step back, he rolled down the alleys, arms lacerated as he fell against the Victorian brickwork.

He finally arrived at his house and entered the rear yard gate, which had been left off the latch. Staggering in to the yard, which measured around seven foot square, his stomach suddenly turned quite literally. It reminds me of an old saying, 'You don't shit on your own doorstep!'

'I nearly did the other night, I had an awful pint int' Feathers.'

Well this guy did shit on his own doorstep albeit, it was quite lucky really, as his underpants saved the red stonework from a pounding.

He realised what he had done immediately and removed his worn shoes and hand-me-down trousers with a care and dexterity never seen in one so drunk. He slipped his pants down his legs as though they were filled with nettles and a broad smile broke the tension in his face realising he had avoided a slip up (or a slip down).

Without any aforethought, he knew what was to be done, as though he had practised the manoeuvre a thousand times in training. Although he had never undertaken or attempted such a feat before, it was to go like a British army exercise …..like clockwork.

Across the yard was an old washing line and in its centre stood a clothes prop raising the middle of the line, to save dirt on the washing. He carefully slid the six-foot prop away from the line and looked for room. Carefully placing the underpants on the forked end of the prop he allowed the foul end to drop back creating a saggy sack of excrement. His actions were akin to a fisherman on the banks of the River Moray, fly fishing for salmon.

With huge effort and a tear rolling down his cheek, stomach aching from the pain of uncontrollable laughter, he launched the straining Y fronts, weighted with their contents high into the night sky. The pants, took on an ambient quality as the moon's rays washed them clean, floating high over 15 back yards to land with a resounding splat at No7.

Desperately trying to control the tears and stomach ache he mounted the step, unlatched the door and went into the house choking on laughs so painful it left him double. Rising the stairs he entered his room which he shared with his brother, put on his pyjamas and giggled his way to sleep.

Next morning was bright and sunny and he awoke at around nine o'clock with a heavy head and face cheeks that crinkled when he yawned from the tears the night before. He waked with the sound of his mother calling him from downstairs.

'Mrs Dunaway is at the door for you. Get yourself up you lazy bastard.' His mum picked up his baby sister, a cigarette dangling from her mouth, and took her into the parlour for her breakfast.

He knew Mrs Dunaway lived at number 7. 'Oh my God!!'

Mrs Dunaway was a lovely old lady in the 80s, salt of the earth with origins in Ireland and still spoke with a heavy accent even though she had moved to England in her teens. He went down the stairs and pulled back the door which had swung partially closed. There was Mrs Dunaway holding her two hands out flat as though she ready to take the host at the local Catholic Church communion. Laid along the withered hands of the old lady was a brilliant white pair of folded Y fronts, freshly washed and, believe it or not, ironed.

'I tink these are yurs.'

Turning purple, he reached out and took the reconditioned pants from her hand.

'How did you know they were mine?' he cried.

'Yer feking name's on the label, ya dirty bastard.'

Another of Simon's famous tales was when he was working for a large conglomerate. The company manufactured paper and related products including toilet rolls and unusually, ladies' tampons. I really do not know how long Simon worked for the company or indeed, why he changed career and went into financial services.

Simon used to visit the whole of the North West as a representative. Old septic knuckles would be a good term for these agents who normally have to knock on hundreds of doors to build up their client base. However, Simon had an established patch which included Liverpool and surrounding district. Simon, being Simon, whenever he had to visit Liverpool knew something would happen and invariably did.

On one occasion, Simon was to visit a supermarket in the middle of a run-down council estate in a rough part of Liverpool. Ensuring his locking wheel nuts were tightly in place with the special tool, Simon prepared for the journey west, down the M62. He had a good run that day with light traffic, and Simon arrived within forty minutes and parked in front of the supermarket. The supermarket was part of a chain in the North West, and whilst not being one of the major players that we all love (or hate), it still had a reasonable reputation at the lower end of retailing.

Simon alighted from the car, locked it and started walking towards the shop. Suddenly he stopped, turned and checked that he had locked the vulnerable company vehicle. Unfortunately the battery was going and he had to walk part way back to the car before it flashed, confirming that he had previously locked it correctly.

Turning back he walked towards the shop once again, pulled the door open and entered. The store was fairly busy, being a Thursday, which traditionally was the busiest day after Saturday, as it coincided with dole day. The women of the house always ensured that the food shop was done before the money was drunk or smoked away.

'Shopping trolley music' was piped through old speakers high in the ceiling and the long isles appeared sparse and under-stocked. Simon sensed that this could be a big order. Maybe this would be a good day after all.

Simon walked down the third aisle which housed kitchenware towards the rear of the store containing the offices. He was just nearing the kitchen foil, plastic cups and cling film when he noticed that the music had been interrupted and a slight hissing noise replaced the innocuous tinkling of strings.

Suddenly, the speakers burst into life, small puffs of dust emanating out with the sound pressure that ensued. 'CUSTOMER ANNOUNCEMENT', boomed through the dust. The voice was a man's, but hardly manly, a high pitched Scouse squeak that sounded like Minni Ripperton on helium, but my God it was loud.

It continued after a very brief pause like a gun-shot report.

'SIMON SMITH, KIMBERLEY CLARKE……..YOU CAN FUCK OFF!'

Simon's left foot was slightly in the air, having not quite completing the step in his gait. He bought it down, swivelled 180 degrees and walked straight out. Maybe the day was not going to be so good after all.

Two other stories originated at the same shop.

Once when Simon was there, he turned the corner of one of the isles to see a very fat woman pushing a pram. She was wearing a base ball hat, huge baggy T shirt sporting the word 'Nike', skin tight black leggings and white trainers. She pushed a pram, however, the seat was devoid of child and he noticed that the sibling was walking four of five yards behind its mother. The child was probably three and a half, dummy in its mouth and mother and tot proceeded towards him.

When the mother was about 10 yards away, she paused at the freezer and started to rummage frantically searching out the best deal on potato alphabites.

Simon was mesmerised and not to appear too nosey pretended to be intrigued by the black forest gateaux in the freezer opposite. Whilst the potato freezer contents were being severely distressed, the child behind the sporty whale pulled down his trousers and pants, squatted, and laid a large log right in the centre of the isle. With the tapered steamer firmly laid, the child pulled its apparel back up to its rightful place and wandered forward to his mum who had decided that the deal of the day was 2 for 1 Potato Faces at £1.29.

'Mummy, mummy look what I've done.' The woman continued to re-arrange the freezer for the best deals, now on value fish fingers and did not look up. If fact she tipped up even higher, the centre of gravity moving from top high to bottom low as her pendulous breast joined the frozen fish below. Her ankles started to rise as she stretched into the icy depths, attempting to reach a bag of 'own brand' that were slightly out of date, knowing she could strike a deal.

The cellulite ballast imprisoned in her leggings strained at the effort, creating a black pitted moonscape where man only once had not feared to tread.

'One small step for man, one giant leap for mankind.' I think not! Grabbing the innocent frozen fingers of fish, the bulk pivoted en masse and scabby ankles resumed their place on terra firma. Pulling down her sporty Nike top, revealing large erect nipples resulting from the icy chill below, she turned and placed her purchases into the trolley.

'Mummy, mummy, look what I've done, look what I've done,' the child repeated and the mother turned to see the newly created mini roundabout in the centre of the frozen food isle. Simon awaited the woman's explosion and implosion of the child's right buttock, however, the woman took the child's hand in hers and with the other hand on the trolley walked away. 'Come on, Tyrone, I need to get some ciggies.'

Many things can be learned from this story - The total lack of responsibility, care and social awareness of certain people in our community, a 'couldn't give a shit' attitude to life, happy allowing others to clean up the mess they create and a dreadful role model for the offspring they produce. How on earth will these kids know any better when they are old enough, not to give a damn? The story also emphasises that some women shouldn't wear leggins and should shop at Iceland, where the freezers are shallower.

The other story concerned the parking for the store. There was a main car park at the back, however, the entrance to the shop was a hundred yards away at the front and those shoppers with cars regularly attempted to park at the front of the shop to avoid undue exercise. A narrow passageway faced the facade, leading onto the local council estate.

Simon was once sitting in his car eating an egg and cress sandwich and a packet of Walkers French Fries for lunch. The road outside the shop had been cordoned off for council workers to apply double yellow lines, hoping to encourage usage of the designated car park, following complaints from residents. Two council workers were employed, one to clean the nearside of the road in preparation of the lines, and the other to push the steaming, wheeled yellow paint pot to create the restriction.

Both men were working, heads down, applying the bitumen in fairly straight lines, working for 10 yards before reversing to create the second tram line. Unbeknown to the men, there was a hoodie shadowing their every move working approximately 20 yards behind them. As the bitumen reached a critical temperature, just before it welded itself to the road surface, it became pliable similar to plastic. As this point was reached, the yobbo turned the start of the line over onto itself, slowly rolling it into a yellow sausage. He continued his work and the roll became arctic in nature (do they still make arctic rolls?), becoming larger and larger each foot. By the time the workers had turned the corner, the two yellow lines were no longer, and behind them, two, two foot yellow liquorice wheels adorned the road side.

Puzzled, and somewhat amused, Simon drove off to his next appointment.

He went back to the shop a few weeks later and saw that, as usual, cars were parked along the front of the shop. Simon wandered in and discussed the affair with the manager.

'Oh they're always doing that,' he said.

'But why?' enquired Simon.

'So they can nick.'

'What do you mean?'

'Well they want cars to park there. When the shoppers walk back to the store to get their pound back for the trolley, they nick the shopping out of the boot and leg it down the passage. Nice bit of tucker for free.'

If anything could go wrong it would with Simon. He was once issued with a new company car. And what car do you think it was? A Ford Mondeo of course. I'm not sure that Simon was particularly proud of his new motor, is one ever proud of a company car? I'm not sure. I suppose that it depends on your disposition. Anyway, Simon took charge of his new motor vehicle and drove it in his work as appointments dictated.

He was working at lot of the time at Bramhall branch and one morning he parked his car in the local car park. He found a space and carefully manoeuvred the car in between the two white lines marking the space. He placed the hand brake and walked to obtain his ticket. He placed the fifty pence piece in the ticket machine and walked back to the car with the ticket, peeled off the back and firmly attached it to the driver's side window. He opened the boot and removed his bag, shut the boot and walked off to the branch for the day's labours.

He returned after a number of appointments, a couple of hours later, to find that the car was no longer in the parking place. It had rolled back some four feet resulting in the two way lane to be blocked sufficiently on one side, so that two cars could not pass one another. He walked to the driver's door and noticed a parking ticket under the windscreen wiper. On the £30 fixed penalty notice, it stated that it had been issued as Simon had not parked the vehicle within a parking bay and the car was deemed an obstruction.

Simon just could not believe how this had happened but paid the ticket fine immediately at the discounted price of £15.

A number of weeks later, he received a letter in the post from Ford stating that there was a problem with their new Mondeo and was subsequently recalling them for alteration. It had been pointed out that there was a major problem with the hand brake. Unfortunately, when Simon had parked the car he had not placed the car into gear and it was on a slight incline. The hand brake had failed completely. It could only happen to Simon!

When he was working for Kimberley Clarke, the salesmen were occasionally allowed to take products home to give out to family and friends and now and again, shops. These were deemed as samples and could be given out to promote the brand name. Simon was given one hundred packets of a new tampon product on the Thursday and was at a family party that evening. He handed out packets of the tampons to the ladies at the party and to various shops and supermarkets on the Friday.

On the Monday, Simon received a call from Head Office stating that there was a major problem with the new product and was potentially dangerous. When the woman wished to change the tampon, the string just detached itself and this could be a fairly serious issue from a medical perspective. Simon then had to re-visit all his family, friends, shops and supermarkets before any one used the tampon and apologise to anyone that had.

One of my favourite stories did not actually involve Simon, albeit, it would have been fairly typical of his luck to have endured this luckless event. However, it did involve another of Simon's colleagues who was due to attend a meeting with four directors of a large company based in city centre, Manchester. It was in the days of those old brief cases which had a bottom like a concertina with a leather flap which came across, with a buckle to fasten the bag shut. All teachers used to have them in the seventies. They were the type that we used to fill with house bricks.

Anyway, this guy needed some money out of his account and went to a cash point in King Street in Manchester. He placed down his bag and took out his wallet from which he pulled his switch card. Placing it into the cash giver, he requested £100 and didn't want a receipt. The card was duly despatched back and finally the 4x£20 and 2x£10 popped out of the machine rather than a Toffee Crisp wrapper. He placed the money into his wallet, picked up his bag and walked down King Street to his appointment a few blocks away.

The sun was shining for once on Manchester and all was fair to middling in the guy's mind. He was not sure of how the meeting would go, however, the finance director was very bullish and positive about a new pension scheme for the company, however, he would have to persuade the other directors as there was obviously cost involved to the company to provide this fringe benefit to the staff of 35.

He walked past the usual high street department stores and headed for the business in question knowing that he was to meet on the twenty third floor of a large office building and the meeting was to take place in the board room. He walked along the street in question overwhelmed by the huge concrete, brick and glass constructions that lined the street. As an aside, I am always amazed whilst walking in a big city. You see a large building on your right and walk past it, but it seems to take an age. Everything is so large and formidable. One, I think, has to get used to a city, or indeed working in a city centre. It is totally different to walking or working in a suburban village or town. It takes so long to get anywhere.

Back to the story! The chap finally found the correct building which soared above him, touching the sky with its glass and steel structure reflecting the blue of the stratosphere above. The architect had created this building from embryonic beginnings, knowing that once it had risen from the ground, it would provide reflection and a mirror like presence, and whilst cold in its material of boiled sand and re-enforced steel, it radiated a glow of warmth into the city. It was majestic in its appearance and the architect had been truly gifted.

He walked through the glass frontage through the revolving doors and approached the security desk. He signed in and clipped the resulting visitor's pass to his lapel and was advised to go to the twenty third floor of the building. He pressed the button of the lift and within seconds the building gave up its amenity allowing access to the sky. He pressed the button for the 23rd floor, slight butterflies in his tummy, knowing that this deal could be the making of him and his pay packet from a substantial bonus if he was able to secure the sign up.

Whilst shooting up to the bluest of skies and the stars beyond, he noticed the push button steel plate which incorporated all the buttons for all the floors, the alarm bell and open and close doors buttons, and within it was the name of the manufacturer of the lift. The manufacturer was a German manufacturer called Schindler. If you look out for them you will see them all over the place mainly in Europe. Schindler's lift!!!

He alighted the lift and walked to the glass doors engraved and emblazoned with the name of the company etched proudly within its toughened glass and he approached a very attractive brunette in her late twenties. Somewhat distracted by her beauty, he fumbled in his jacket pocket for the letter to identify the names of his audience and advised the beauty of his appointment. She forwarded him to the waiting area and offered him a coffee which he declined.

After approximately five minutes the stunning model receptionist asked him to follow her to the board room where the meeting would take place with the finance director, the managing director and two of the other key players in the company. His heart started racing, testosterone and adrenaline pumping through his veins, a hunting dog, the scent of its prey full in his nostrils.

In the room the woman left and he placed his bag on the huge solid oak and mahogany inlaid polished table that stretched in front of him. Almost twenty people could sit around this table with ease and he marvelled at its quality and obvious value. The last time Queen Anne legs like that had been inspected, it had been undertaken by Arthur Negus. His commission had suddenly increased to such a degree that he would not have to do another deal all year and still be top performer.

The four directors walked in together, their sternness and formality obvious and he was suddenly aware that he had left his bag on the polished, antique, endless table. He shook the hand of the four before he had chance to move the bag but was very conscious of its presence, and so were the directors.

The four directors sat down two on each side and the chap, just prior to sitting down, pulled his bag across the table and placed it on the floor. Upon the mahogany inlay of polished beauty stood the largest dog turd ever seen in living memory. The table not only enjoyed the beautiful form of the perfect stool but also where the bag had been dragged was a trail of faeces, like the arc of a comet, textured, and varying in quality and density of brown, black and yellow shit.

All five looked at the modern art, akin to a Turner prize at the Tate Gallery. No one spoke, everyone smelled.

Five stomachs turned, in various states of unsettlement. The finance director started to swallow quickly, obviously attempting not to heave in front of his fellow directors.

'I think we need to re-arrange the appointment,' the managing director belched, gulping for breath as the dark rainbow emitted its full fragrance on the room and all four stood up and left as one, as they had entered.

The offending stool emanated from the largest dog ever to have walked through Manchester and more than likely had a small barrel of brandy attached to its neck. When the guy placed the concertina bag down at the cash point, he had laid one of the folds of the bottom of the bag straight onto the offending turd.

It had stuck out at the front akin to an inverted periscope on a submarine and had caught his trousers on a number of occasions during his walk to the meeting. Walking back to the reception he noticed that there was dog shit all over the chair that he had sat at in the reception area and another blob attached to the steel lift exit.

I have no idea whether he himself cleaned up the offending deposits or just left the offices in the speediest manner ever, leaving the beautiful brunette to clean up the mess in her Marigold gloves. There is something quite sexy about Marigolds and I could think of something else I could do with a beautiful brunette in them but we will not go there at this stage.

I have no idea whether the chap ever went back to the company and if so, whether he was very careful where he stood or placed his bag on the way there.

However, I somehow doubt that the guy signed up the pension policy even though deposits were left.

CHAPTER EIGHT:

Odd things happen abroad

The body repeats the landscape. They are the source of each other and create each other - Meridel Le Sueur

The vast majority of holidays I have enjoyed in life have either been in arctic conditions in the French Alps, or with groups of mates on very long spoiled walks on the golf course. My great love of skiing was developed following the introduction to the sport to me by Rosa when I was 24, and we have endeavoured to go at least once a year ever since. Our children Daniel and David have also learned from the ages of three and are depressingly good. It is a strange feeling when your children become better at something than you are; it is also extremely fulfilling. As an aside, the day your child first tells you something you did not know is a powerful moment in any parent's life, and one to be savoured.

We have never really had many misfortunes, accidents or unhappy memories on any holiday, touch wood, other than the travel to or from the destination in question.

The first ski holiday I went on was to Artesina, a comparatively small ski resort in Italy where Rosa's uncle had a small apartment. Isn't it funny, when a pilot of a commercial airliner states that due to a certain reason, something unexpected will happen which will mean an additional time delay to the journey of twenty minutes, you feel happy in the knowledge that it will only delay the journey by twenty minutes.

On the flight to Italy we were destined to fly to Turin. 'Ladies and gentlemen, boys and girls, this is your captain speaking. Unfortunately, due to fog at Turin we have to re-direct our flight to Milan Malpensa Airport. This will delay the landing of the aircraft by a period of 20 minutes and Thompson holidays apologises for any inconvenience.'

The only trouble was that we were not on a Thompson Holiday, (we had only booked a flight through them), and Malpensa is over one hundred miles from Turin where we were to be met by Rosa's uncle to be driven to his apartment.

Upon arrival at Milan, we were told to wait for the coaches to collect us to take us to our respective resorts however, we needed to go to Turin Airport. The Thompson reps did not enjoy the Southern Comfort induced foul mouth tirade that came inappropriately out of the Sheardie mouth. I regret to this day, one, that children and those of a quiet disposition were present during the oration in front of hundreds, and two, the word I called her, which is a word far more prevalently used in London than in the sticks. Maybe it was a pertinent word derived from the Southern part of the Comfort I gained from the verbal abuse.

The twenty minutes detour resulted in a change of plan and we decided to attempt to travel to Rosa's uncle's house in Savona on the Liguria Riviera from which he would then transport us the following day to the ski resort.

So for an extra 20 minutes on a plane the following other forms of travel, pain and suffering had to be endured. It commenced with a very pleasurable overnight sit in a blue plastic chair in the airport, a true testament to the body's ability to cope with the pain of piles. Malpensa shuts at night and we were the only people there other than men with very large guns!

At 7.00 a.m. we endured a local bus ride enjoying the delights of the Scorpion's 'Rock you like a Hurricane' on full blast, to a local suburban train station. Bear in mind we had hand luggage incorporating duty free goods, (minus half a bottle of Southern Comfort-that made it a little bit lighter anyway), two suitcases, two boot bags and two pairs of skis in ski bags.

We waited at the train station with all the commuters who looked at us as though we were from the local acute mental ward. Rosa boarded the train whilst I threw each of the pieces of luggage up the steps to her. Everything was aboard and safely stored on the train as it set off, other than me. My embarkation became the benchmark for the Indiana Jones and the Temple of Doom stunt scenes as I beat Linford Christie's world record 100 metres time down the platform, to jump on at the back.

At Milan we then discovered that we had arrived at the wrong station for the connection. We jumped a taxi rank of 57 Italian studs and studesses at Milano Lambrate station and asked to be taken to Milano Centrale Station by the taxi driver who had to sit in the passenger seat as

I had boarded the car on the drivers side - I had even put my seat belt on for God's sake!

Once re-seated appropriately, we were driven to the correct station and waited one and a half hours for the train to Genova. From Genova station we waited another hour for the link to Savona to be met by Rosa's uncle to take us back to his house. The journey had taken thirty hours and we were still 150 miles from the resort. We finally arrived the following day after an evening of rest and more Southern Comfort, 48 hours behind schedule.

On another holiday with our great friends the Kearys, we left Geneva airport with the captain stating that we would be hanging a right straight after take-off, blah, blah, blah. The plane took off and before the seat belt signs went out, a ball of flame shot out of the right engine and we took a left, straight back to Geneva where we arrived with all emergency crews scrambled. I have never experienced a landing where as you approach, looking through the porthole you see lines of ambulances, fire brigade engines and other such like vehicles, with blue lights, throbbing disco arcs in the blackness. Positively scary! We landed and had to wait in the departure lounge for three hours whilst they pulled the offending large gull out of the Rolls Royce engine. A bird in the fins is worth three in the lounge.

On another holiday we skied in Chamonix in the French Alps. On the way there, Ged had bought a selection of articles from the WH Smith outlet in the airport departure lounge. These included a Times newspaper, a pack of playing cards and a Travel Scrabble, together with an assortment of wine gum type sweets all contained in a bag, with the WH Smith logo emblazoned on the side.

On the plane, he had placed the bag under his seat upon departure and forgot to retrieve the bag of goodies, only realising when we had cleared customs. He wasn't particularly bothered about the Times or the Travel Scrabble or the cards but having an unhealthy wine gum addiction and, in the knowledge that Bassetts do not export to French sweet shops, he was panic stricken.

We had to wait for the southern jessies to arrive half an hour later from Gatwick to fill the transfer coach to the resort and he and I therefore had a few minutes to kill. We decided to set off to try to retrieve the bag via the information desk.

What you must understand is that neither Ged or I have ever booked any of the holidays we have ever enjoyed as families together, as the trawling of brochures and the many enquiring phone calls were always undertaken by our wives. They are brilliant at choosing great resorts with accommodation on the slopes – well that is our excuse – we can't really be arsed where we go as long as we have a good time.

We trotted down the three steps of the coach whilst the girls were adjusting their phones to a French phone company, and looked for the signs for the information desk. This was a largish separate room from the main concourse and we entered via large glass doors. In front of us were three reception desks, however, only one was manned. The only other people in the room were military police with large machine guns dressed in blue combat gear and other formal security staff dressed appropriately in black trousers and white shirts.

We approached the manned desk to be greeted by one of the most stunning women you have ever seen. She was pristinely dressed in the Air France livery, auburn hair tied up in an intricate manner, was stunningly bronzed, with a face from the cover of the Tatler magazine. She really was beautiful.

She looked up at us, smiled and in the sexiest voice ever said, 'Bonjour messieurs, Comme je peux vous aider?'

Ged turned and looked at me, a small glint of a smile came to his face. I couldn't interpret the acknowledgement as to whether he was smiling at her infinite beauty, knowing that I was thinking the same, or he didn't understand a word she had said. I was smiling at both and knew Ged well enough to know he was thinking both. I was certainly smiling at her infinite beauty and didn't understand a word she had said.

'Doo yoo speekie English?' enquired Ged. Ged has a habit of speaking with broken French English, whenever he speaks to any French person, and it has to be said that it sounds quite ridiculous. I think he likes to think he is the policeman in 'Ello Ello'.

'I was just pissing,' was his favourite catchphrase.

'Say what you see, see what you see!' Oh no! That is Catchphrase and was Roy Walker's.

The French beauty said in perfect English that she did and how could she help us.

'I left a bag on the plane under the seat,' replied Ged.

'Which flight were you on?'

Ged looked at me and smiled, and then back at her.

'I don't know.' He looked at me again and shrugged his shoulders feeling a little foolish that he didn't know where he had come from. Trouble is I didn't know the flight number either and I shrugged back, starting to laugh.

'Where did you fly from?' asked the beauty.

'England!' came the response. I continued to laugh and I saw Ged's eyes starting to water.

'Which city in England?' stated the impeccably dressed native of the French land, seemingly polite but starting to become a little impatient at the seeming lack of intelligence and knowledge of the two Brits abroad in front of her.

'Oh! Sorry, Manchester,' Ged replied, a tear appearing from the corner of his left eye.

'And what was in the bag?' enquired Marie Antoinette.

Ged looked at me and I was starting to belly ache with laughter as the conversation degenerated but attempted to maintain some semblance of dignity and composure as a representative of our great nation. A tear ran down Ged's left cheek as he realised the seriousness and repercussion of the answer.

'Well, there was a Travel Scrabble...'

I laughed out loud.

'...a Times Newspaper, some playing cards and two packets of wine gums,' Ged spluttered, tears starting to roll down his cheeks on both sides now. I was hurting with the pain of stifled laughter and almost doubled up turning away from the desk as I could stand the conversation no more.

'And where are you staying in France?' asked Eugenie de Montijo, the last Empress of France.

Ged looked at me and I looked at Ged and we both knew that each other didn't know.

'Em, somewhere in the French Alps, I think.'

Marguerite de Valois, Queen Consort of Navarre, amazingly retained her composure as these two imbeciles crying in front of her struggled to speak or even make eye contact through the tears streaming down their faces. How had the English ever won at the Battle of Agincourt?

At that point, whether it was down to the long sit on the plane or my stomach cramps from the laughter, my body gave in to the hilarity of this ridiculous conversation. I could take the pain of hysteria no more. Without warning or any control or ability to evade or stall, I let out a huge explosion of a fart.

There was total silence. The whole world had ceased to breathe at that instant. Nature was frozen for a nanosecond. All of God's living creatures from the Rhetus Periander butterfly in Peru, to the Blue Whales in the North Pacific paused in flight.

Within an instant, the world resumed its orbit around the sun, but momentarily in slow motion. The French beauty's eyes moved at a snail's pace across the room towards my puce red face, as the combated soldiers turned, heightened awareness, trigger fingers raised from the safety catches of their weapons. Other security workers just froze as though the Magic Boomerang had been thrown.

'Oh! Just don't worry about it,' stuttered Ged and we both turned towards the opposite door we had entered. We walked, doubled up in the ecstasy and agony of uncontrollable giggles, hardly able to breathe, or see through the tears.

'Halt!'

The soldier's brusque and firm command was in total contrast to the gentle, soothing, broken dialect that had emitted from the perfect mouth of the Princess. We almost stopped laughing. He pointed to the doors opposite from whence we had come, as we were heading for the doors leading to the interrogation room where they torture British holiday makers.

By the way, the Brits under the command of Henry V of England stuffed the Froggies captained by Charles d'Abret at Agincourt on Friday 25th October 1415. Part of the 100 years war, we drubbed them as a result of our use of Longbow men. Our army comprised 5,900 whilst the frogs had an enormous 20,000 to 30,000 at their disposal. We lost 112 men whilst they lost between 7,000 and 10,000. If a Longbow man was captured by the French it was ordered that both fore finger and middle finger be cut off in order that they could no longer pull back the bow string. Hence the V sign that we all use today in defiance. Why they didn't just cut their heads off instead, I do not know? Maybe that's also why we won! Any countryman who eats frogs' legs and snails out of choice must be somewhat lacking in the brain department. And who tried it first?

I have to say that Ged and I appear to be buffoons in certain situations and you would probably concur, however, we are both fairly intelligent people and our downfall is often that we are a little too laid back for our own good, particularly when holidays are concerned. It was maybe just that vacation, but we managed to continue the trend to some degree and the girls, Rosa and Julie, on occasion, joined our merry band of court jesters.

On the third day of the holiday the two families had been skiing all day and had a fantastic time. The weather was simply stunning with blue, azure skies, snow capped peaks and perfectly groomed pistes. It was late in the afternoon and Ged, Julie, their children and I, decided not to ski down the mountain back to the resort, but to catch an eight man Gondola to descend the 1500 metres, whilst the rest of my family continued to ski. A beer was calling me from afar and it had my name written all over it!

These types of lifts, for the uninitiated comprise, what can only be described as, a large glass and steel bubble which catches onto a cable. The cable forms a complete circle and passes through two stations, one at the bottom of the mountain and one at the top and uses a diversion pulley system within the station, to slow the cabin down, and open and shut the doors to allow foot flow. This particular bubble had room for eight standing and had two identical racks on the outside in which to slide in your skis. Once this was done you entered the cabin and the doors automatically closed behind you, to either (and more usually), travel up the mountain, or for sightseers or those too knackered to face a final descent, travel down. I wouldn't say that you have to be really quick at 'posting' your skies into the rack and enter but there is always a little bit of a scramble, particularly if your posting isn't as efficient as could be.

The Sheardie family 'sans' me skied off into the distance whilst the six of us went into the top station to catch the bubble down. I was lagging behind a little as I had said goodbye to my loved ones, telling them to be safe and Ged and his family arrived before me.

As I was entering the station, the Kearys were starting to board the lift, firstly Julie, then the children and then Ged. Every one of them had taken at least two goes to plant their skis into the holders and time was running out before the bubble would catch on the cable, the doors would shut and they would be whisked away to the land of après ski, beer and reflection on the day's events.

In the increasing panic to embark the whole family were pushing and shoving in utter confusion. Irate words from weary bodies muttered, and Ged, ignoring the furore, was last in. Just! However, just as the doors were shutting he slipped on the ice left from the family's ski boots. One leg went forward and the other backwards and he fell to his side onto the steel floor. Whilst not hurt, he was momentarily stunned and in that second, the doors closed, the mechanism caught the cable, and the bubble was off.

Almost immediately, the whole lift shut down and I could see thirty telecabines swinging at a standstill down the mountain, as the system's safety device kicked in. I had already boarded the following bubble and looking forward through the window of my glass box, was the Keary's, one hundred feet above the ground, stopped, rocking from side to side. Trapped in the automatic doors which were unable to close was one Nordica rear entry blue ski boot facing upwards. No part of a leg was visible, just the whole of a Nordica rear entry boot.

It took approximately five minutes for the station engineers to manually back up the cable onto the releasing mechanism to open the doors, whilst all that time Ged was lying on the floor, surrounded by a totally embarrassed family, with all his body inside and his foot and boot outside. You could almost taste the frustration and irritation of the hundreds of skiers in bubbles coming up the mountain for a final run. I was laughing so much I weed my pants. A telephone call was made from the top station to the bottom station, an alarm was triggered and the system recommenced its work. The Keary bubble catapulted out of the bay devoid of any additional exterior appendage, closely followed by mine.

I was alone in my pod waving at the Kearys one hundred feet in front. The whole family had their hands held in front of their faces in disgrace, protecting their identities from the skiers in the bubbles going upwards, other than Ged. He appeared to be also crying with laughter and, no doubt, wet his pants as well. I could see Julie giving him a real ear bashing as the descent continued. However, this was not the end of the story.

The two bubbles continued at their rapid progress down the mountain for approximately seven minutes and the base station appeared larger and larger with every second. The hapless Keary bubble swung into the entrance and picked up the unlocking mechanism, the doors swinging open as my bubble was entering the building. Julie was first out. However, she was not on her feet, but in the air, impersonating a child's first attempt at a dive into a swimming pool. She had tripped over Ged's blue, rear entry Nordica ski boot in an attempt to exit rapidly and escape the culprit who had caused her so much embarrassment. Julie literally, front rolled out of the pod into metal railings, there to control the flow of users of the lift.

The engineers at the bottom lift immediately pressed the large red emergency button and the lift instantaneously stopped. They rushed over to Julie to ensure that she had not sustained injury whilst the rest of the family slowly disembarked, Ged bringing up the rear. Whilst he was obviously concerned for his wife's welfare, I could see that once that had been positively confirmed, his eyes filled up with the tears of hysteria.

He told me later that he had nearly pooed in his pants. I later told him that I had. I would never expect such an experience to happen again in Courcheval 1850. Indeed I don't expect that it will ever occur again in any ski resort around the world. One blue, rear entry, Nordica boot had caused a telecabine emergency failure at both the top and bottom stations.

Just as an aside, it was not to be the last occasion those infamous boots caused rip roaring jocularity. On another late afternoon, we had all headed for the nearest bar and taken refuge in a small corner of the busy hostelry. Ged had had a problem with his boots that day and they had been rubbing, causing some pain in both calf muscles. As a result, he had taken the opportunity to take both boots off to allow some circulation back into the weary muscles, and was resting his stockinged feet on the table in front.

I have to say that we probably had a few too many and Ged, who is not a big drinker at all, was feeling somewhat wobbly. It was time to return to our catered chalet to shit, shower and shave, (and that was just the women), prior to dinner. The girls and children went off to stake their claim on the use of the lavatory and the limited hot water that was to be available that evening. I waited for Ged to put on his boots.

We walked out of the bar and headed home and I couldn't understand what the strange noise was emitting from Ged's legs, a chinking of metal on metal. I looked down at his blue, rear entry, Nordica boots which were unfastened. He had placed them on the wrong feet and the buckles were catching as he was walking.

There were two other experiences on that particular holiday that I recall, one with amusement and the other with sheer embarrassment. We were playing a board game which involved asking questions to individuals. Rosa was asked,

'When do chickens lay their eggs?'

She replied, 'In the Spring.'

This woman is an education consultant for a local authority and we wonder why the country is going to rack and ruin.

The other involved my son David and he was around five at the time. The two families were staying at a catered chalet which basically means that the chalet girls would prepare all meals, make the beds etc. She would also eat with you in the evenings. David and William, Ged's son, were watching a film on a portable CD television prior to dinner, and unfortunately, we had not realised that the film in question was a fifteen certificate. I know, I know, we should be ashamed of ourselves. It only came to our attention when we heard various swear words such as shit and bastard that we immediately ejected the offending disk of silver to replace it for something a little more akin to their age.

We all sat down to dinner with the chalet girl, whose name escapes me, and she served up a delicious starter followed by an equally mouth watering main, comprising ingredients obtained and cooked according to the local traditions of the Savoie region of which the French Alps forms a part. It was gourmet cooking at its finest. We were stuffed, happy, laughing and all were content.

'Would you like some more, David?' the plain, yet jolly maid enquired.

'No thanks, you whore!' he replied, an innocent smile on his sun kissed face.

I have never experienced seeing nine jaws literally drop to the table. It could have been a recreation out of a cartoon film, or Jim Carey, just being Jim Carey. David, of course was chastised, however, he had no idea what the noun referred to and what tumultuous implications this labelling could have had to the young girl of alleged ill repute.

Apparently she went out on the streets soliciting later that evening, and earned €39.10. 'Who gave you the ten cents?' the chap asked. 'They all did!' came the response. She took it in good spirit and emphasises the old chestnut that you should never work with animals or children.

Have you ever missed a flight? Many frequent flyers would say yes! Have you ever missed a flight on one of the busiest flying days of the year, February half term Saturday, incorporating Valentine's Day? Flights are always difficult to obtain late on that particular day and the carriers had put on a number of extra flights. The flight back from Lyon was at 3.30 am on the following Sunday and we therefore presumed that the flight out would be the Sunday also. It wasn't and I realised when I tried to book the taxi on the Saturday afternoon, to take us to the Airport, for 1.30 a.m. Only trouble was that the plane had left 7 hours ago.

The holiday in question was rather expensive in the French Alps in a catered chalet and was costing circa £2,800 for the week. We frantically contacted our agent, Thomas Cook, who were absolutely brilliant. There were no flights to Lyon with any seats whatsoever until the following Tuesday. The lady from Thomas Cooks spent hours searching for alternatives and eventually found an answer. However, it was to prove very costly.

The following day we left for the Airport at 10.00 a.m. We flew first class from Manchester to Charles de Gaulle in Paris. I've never had champagne before whilst taxiing down runway number one. At Charles De Gaulle we went in the VIP room and raided just about every free item on offer much to the disgust of the Japanese businessmen with their newly invented laptops and foreign dignitaries en masse. Considering that in years to come I was to be labelled an alcoholic, this was a treasure trove. To my children, later to find out they were chocoholics, this was a treasure trove. To Rosa, later to find out that she was a wet wipe, soap, free sample perfume, and giftaholic, this was treasure trove.

We flew on from Paris to Lyon on an internal flight and upon disembarkation went to the taxi rank. There were around ten taxis waiting and no one in the queue.

'Single trip quote for La Plagne, if you please driver.'

'That is two hundred and twenty kilometres away,' said the first, wiping his brow, knowing that he was at the end of his shift. He took the fare anyway. We arrived 24 hours late and had cost us an additional £1,000 including a £180 taxi fare. The moral of this story is to always check your tickets and never fly with the Sheards.

The second and third ski trips I went on were with 28 schoolchildren from a local high school, where Rosa was the senior girls PE teacher. Whilst it appears that this would be a good method of learning to ski with fairly little cost (as the teacher's holiday costs were usually covered in part by the tour operator), in fact little skiing was done, mainly as the children, of course, came first.

They had to be shepherded to every lesson and collected afterwards. Even the evenings the teachers and helpers were, in essence, baby sitters having to do rounds of the bedrooms to ensure that the boys were in their rooms and the girls in theirs. There was obviously always major concerns that the two groups would intermingle and worries that we would come back from the holiday with 29, albeit, one in an embryonic stage.

I heard one story from a teacher at another school that they had taken a trip the previous year and one of their siblings had chatted to a fourteen year old boy on the plane. He attended a different school, however it transpired that both schools were to reside at the same hotel.

The teachers of the two schools, one a boy's comprehensive, and the other a girl's private school, allocated bedrooms upon arrival at 1.00 p.m. At 1.25 p.m. the teacher from the girl's school checked that each of her charges were unpacking whereupon she found the 14 year old girl in bed with the boy she had met on the plane, legs akimbo, both totally naked. They had even taken off their ski goggles! He must have had some great chat up lines, either that or she must have had!! Both could chat more about their sexual encounter the following day at length in the airport lounge, whilst awaiting their flights home in utter and total disgrace.

On one of these holidays, we took the pupils to a resort in Italy. This was the middle of February and although the resort was low it had a reasonable track record for the white stuff. However, not one flake had been produced by our Good Lord that season, and the snow plains were lush green with barren outcrops of rocks and crags basking in the winter sunshine. The tour operator guaranteed snow or faced a heavy penalty chargeback, and therefore every morning the children were awoken at 6.00 a.m., breakfasted, and placed on a coach at 7.30 a.m. Thirty two pairs of boots, skies and poles were loaded in the cargo bay. The coach then departed on its daily three hour coach journey to another resort which enjoyed snow making facilities.

After a two hour lesson, a two hour lunch break, and a further two hour lesson in the afternoon, all skis, boots and poles were reloaded for the three hour coach journey back. We did this for seven straight days and bearing in mind that the adults were the first to awake and last to bed after countless drinks until 3.00 a.m. it was the most gruelling trip ever.

Having said that, the kids knew no different as this was the first skiing holiday most had enjoyed and they thought that this was the norm. It just shows that children are not only hardy creatures but also adapt and enjoy life at face value. There was not one complaint from them the whole holiday and all thought the trip was brilliant.

We used to take the trips with some good friends Arthur and Alma. Arthur was the technology teacher at Rosa's school and we all became close over the years, however, we have now lost contact following Arthur's change in occupation. Arthur was a fun, convivial guy with a wicked sense of humour and enjoyed the Devil's brew as much, if not more in those days, than I did. He always started each holiday with a fairly strict attitude towards discipline, standards and expectation of the children's behaviour whilst on the trip.

'You are representing yourselves, your school and your country, on this trip and we (the teachers and adult support) want to be so proud of you that you have not let us down.'

The seeds of expectation had been firmly implanted and in view of the dangers associated with the sport, the need for discipline and subsequent behaviour was very important.

A year later we were asked to accompany the Bells on a fully paid 'taster trip', laid on by a new school tour operator who wished to show us a whistle stop tour of some Austrian resorts he was to introduce to the brochure the following year, hoping that we would book through his company. The trip for the four of us involved four days of travelling through the Austrian Tyrol sampling resorts and we visited around six over the four days.

We were staying in a hotel with a party of school children of mixed ages from another part of the country and all was going well until the third evening. This was a time before mobile phones and Alma left the hotel during dinner to make a phone call home from a pay phone situated approximately 100 metres from the entrance. Approximately ten minutes later she came back in floods of tears stating that a couple of youngsters, approximately 14 years old, had told the old bitch to get off the fucking phone because they wanted to use it. Arthur was an inside centre for a local rugby club's fourth team and had been captain for many years. As such he wasn't the retiring type and rather than say, 'Oh! The youth of today, they aren't what they used to be and have despicable manners to a gracious lady such as yourself, my darling,' downed his sixth half litre of lager in one and asked me to follow him. I had just arrived back from the gents and had no idea what was going on.

We walked up the road, with Arthur approximately five yards ahead of me, striding out, his intentions clear. I asked him what this was all about and he appraised me of the situation and that in no uncertain words he was going to tell the little shit what he thought of him.

The phone box was on the left hand side of the road and was screened by a row of small conifers, approximately seven feet in height, fairly packed together. We rounded the evergreens and a group of five, fourteen to fifteen year olds were either in or around the front of the phone box. Arthur asked them if a woman had been there a few moments ago and one spouted up that she was on the phone for 'fucking ages'.

Ski wear is intrinsically designed to keep out the bitter cold and permafrost that nature's severe weather can bring. The mountains can be a frigid place with deathly freezing conditions and a truly dangerous place for the unwary or the un-witted. Ski jackets, particularly expensive ones, are normally tough and durable, made from Gortex and lined with insulation to keep out the tearing and maddening bitter wind, snow and sleet.

For the fourteen year old boy, this mountain was the most frightening place on the planet, not from the exposure to nature at its most severe, indeed this chap would have preferred it if he had been totally stark naked on the peak of the 3,000 metre giant glacial peak that formed a dark, foreboding backdrop against the moonlight. This mountain was now a truly dangerous place and even nature's wrath was more welcome than the seething psychopath that stood before him, fists clenched by his side, blood pounding through veins contorted to their limits.

Unfortunately, the boy was not wearing the latest £600 Spyder, top of the range, designer jacket but a £49.99 red C&A budget bargain basement. With all due respect to C&A, and to the Indonesia sweat shop worker who produced it for £4.50 and 50p wages, it stood up to the impending violent attack, beset by the aggrieved spouse.

The jacket was zipped to the top and Arthur, with overwhelming fury, grabbed hold of the bulky breast pockets lifting the terrified victim inches from the ground. He turned ninety degrees to his left and promptly launched the foul mouth towards the hedge with such astounding fury, that the boy went straight through the tightly packed greenery, approximately four feet higher than the ground.

The girl chavs with the transgressor started to scream as Arthur, in a new rugby training ground manoeuvre, launched himself, akin to superman, through the resulting hole left by the human projectile and landed a full body slam onto the orator of abuse with such force that the boy was totally winded.

I ran around the small copse to see Arthur, left fist garrotting the urchin with the throat of his jacket pointing his right forefinger towards the terrified eyes. Arthur only said one thing to the hapless schoolchild. '

'You are representing yourself, your school and your country.'

As Rudyard Kipling once said, 'All the people like us are we, and everyone else is They.'

CHAPTER NINE:

Reflections In The Darkest of Minds – The very grumpy bit!

If the only tool you have is a hammer, you tend to see every problem as a nail – Abraham Maslow

In July 2008 it was estimated that there were 6,706,993,152 individual souls on this beautiful land we call Earth. It makes me smile that this information provided via a search engine is an estimate. You would at least have thought that it would have been rounded off to the nearest 1000. And who are the two?

Our world is stunning. Take a moment to relish it. The hues and glorious colours of the sky at sunset; the beauty of nature, with its animal, reptile and fish life; mountains, glens, rivers and streams and stunning scenery in every corner of every land; the smells and aromas of flora and fauna, weather with its colossal power; a total macrocosm under the sea which covers 70% of our planet. Our world is a utopia, a heaven blessed by the Gods, and we should respect and cherish our opportunity to see, touch, feel, smell and taste it. The world has developed a delicate balance to ensure its own sustainability.

However, I truly believe that mankind has ruined our planet. We are just custodians of our stunning world and each of us live for a nanosecond in the grand scheme of things. Yet, we abuse our residency, ruining the atmosphere with man- made pollution over-turning billions of years of evolution.

We cannot even live with one another. The sick, violent and compassionless way we abuse each other is quite staggering. I was going to describe man's inhumane treatment of fellow man as 'bestial'. However, even animals show less evil intent than some homo sapiens. We kill for the sake of killing, whereas all other animals kill as part of a food chain. How can one man cut the arms off a baby just because it belongs to another tribe? How can one ever endorse the genocide and extermination of part of the population as they believe in a different God? As a race, as beings, with relative high intelligence, we should be totally ashamed.

Humankind in many aspects is driven by greed, envy and jealousy. Many individuals manipulate and dominate for greed's sake. Certain countries and their leaders believe that the world should be run in a certain way and impose those ways on the rest. A fascist state is one that adopts a political theory advocating an authoritarian hierarchical government. Whilst this is not evidenced within those countries per se, and their leaders go out of their way to advocate democratic principles, it is the way in which those governments inflict their control and influences over other countries and their people just because they have different agendas and priorities.

This air of superiority is not born from anything other than greed... or fear.

What makes a wealthy American citizen believe that he or she is better and superior to a tribesman living in the deepest jungle rainforest? No one is any better than anybody else. Every-one on this planet is equal. We all can feel scared, love, hurt, cry, laugh. We all enter this world with no conception of what life will offer. None of us have any say in our colour, creed, gender, disability or sexual leaning. It is inherent. Yet some governments and leaders appear to believe that their way, their principles, scruples and ideals are right and want to impose their views on everyone else. Who is to say that one view is more right than another when we are all equals? George Orwell penned the idiom, 'All people are equal but some are more equal than others.' How true this appears to be in some men's eyes.

Live and let live!

I know! Sheardie is on his high horse. I've mounted my soap box and no Persil advertisement will force me down from it until I've had my say. It's a reason to write a book. You can state your view and the reader has the choice to use the pages to set the fire, or read on. You also can't be punched in the face as you are not imparting your view personally. On the basis that you haven't used the pages to light the Aga I will continue. To those that just have, I hope it burns your house down!

We elect politicians to speak on our behalf. However, when a member of our community is elected, they appear to lose all moral scruples and act, not on behalf of the people who gave them their job in the first place, but for themselves. It is a very exclusive club and once you have joined it, you can virtually do whatever you want to promote your own wealth and notoriety. The vast majority of these self-important tricksters end up just appearing to promote their own infamy, through dropping a bullock,

They also never answer a bloody question! Have you ever noticed? They are groomed in this to such a degree that politician's verse is almost a language in itself.

'Mr Smith, you said, following the Select Committee's findings, that you would address the issue of MP's second home allowance.'

'What, I can say......'

'Let me tell you this....'

The first response means, 'I can't answer your question because I know we haven't', 'I've been told not to' or 'I just want to emphasise certain aspects which will benefit me or my party.'

The second response means, ' Whatever I say in the next few words answers your question and is totally right and should not be questioned.'

Members of Parliament should never forget why they are there, and,

'Let me say this!!!'

They are there to represent the people who elected them. That does not mean that they can purchase a bath plug for 88p or two pornographic films for £10.00 at our expense. What a complete and utter scandal. What's more, it is even more outrageous that they appear unaccountable and can-not be ousted from their position until they themselves call an election. How many other jobs are there where *you* can instigate a contractual letter of employment for a set length of time, and stay on the payroll for that period, irrespective of your ability, morality or honesty?

'Hi Steve! Are you still working in the Bank?'

'Yes! I've been busy lending money. I've also made the local headlines recently.'

'Oh! Why's that?'

'I was found naked on Hampsted Heath indulging in a lewd act with a fifteen year old rent boy. I paid him with money I stole from my customers!'

'Oh, really! Nice to know your position in the company is safe during this economic downturn.'

The United Kingdom, once a truly great nation has gone to pot. We believe as a nation that we still rule the world, whilst we are the laughing stock, the butt of other country's jokes and irritate in the way we suck up to those across the pond. We, as a Nation, appear to have forgotten how to make decisions for ourselves. It makes my blood boil reading daily of the actions taken by institutions and councils, businesses and officials, to ensure that we remain 'politically correct'.

We are no longer able to call Christmas, 'Christmas', for the fear that it may upset someone from another ethnic background. We can't call Easter, 'Easter', for fear of upsetting some in our country, yet we openly allow Eid ul Fitr and Eid ul Adha for our Moslem community and Diwali, Holi, and Durga Puja for the Hindu community. We also see advertisements strewn all over the Chinese community to celebrate their New Year.

If I went over to another country, I would expect to adhere to their rules, cultural and religious beliefs and tolerances. Why therefore, are we not allowed to have our own very long standing traditions, way of life and religion accepted by others, without having to worry about what we call them? It's called Christmas and it's called Easter and we celebrate it. Live with it and shut the fuck up!

It does remind me of the old adage. 'If you don't like it here, sod off somewhere where you do!' Many people think it but nobody has the balls to say it. One would be branded racist. Is it not racist to deny a white Christian the ability to celebrate the birth or sacrifice and resurrection of Jesus Christ? Live and let live. Most people do – why can't all?

Human rights legislation is just barmy and totally irritating. Whilst its origins were very well intended and has protected millions in the past, the interpretation in legal precedents has taken the act to new heights of buffoonery.

The burglar, who has the shit kicked out of him by the occupier of the house he is attempting to steal from, appears to have far more rights under the law than the victim. The scumbag should not be there in the first place and when he sets foot illegally through that door or window he has forced he should expect to get what he receives if he is caught.

He knows that he will not be punished by our pathetic legal system, once the envy of the world, and be let off with a caution or a few hours of community service. I have total respect, admiration and support for anyone taking those matters in to their own hands.

If you are strong enough and brave enough to kick the shit out of those who are robbing your house, do it, do it well and with total conviction. So much so, when they are lying in the hospital bed with two broken legs and three hundred stitches in their brain dead face, they wonder whether they should have taken up a different occupation.

We, in this country are too soft, wet and woolly and have not one vertebra in our cultural backbone. Let's not upset anyone, and everyone will respect us and love us for it. What a load of tosh. It's about time we remembered what our fathers and grandfathers fought for in the great wars and what a great nation we once were. We are fined for placing our wheelie bins out a day early but paedophiles found with sick perverse images of children under ten can get away with signing a register and painting a few fences for fifty hours. We are living in one mad world.

Are we surprised that there are vast swathes of illegal immigrants queuing up in Calais waiting to subscribe to the great gravy train. This country is seen as easy pickings and its subculture believe they have a right to be provided for. You and I pay significant taxes all our lives for some scroat, whether home-bred or not, to be homed, clothed and fed. 'It is their right' because we work and they can't be bothered. Just get a job you lazy bastards and stop relying on the vast majority of decent citizens to bail you out.

Under no circumstances am I saying that every person who claims state handouts is unworthy. Many people are genuine and attempt to find work at every opportunity to support themselves and their families. However, many just cannot be bothered or motivated to seek work. Every person on benefits who has not sought work for a set period should have to do something for the community, maybe pick up litter or clean graffiti before they receive their fortnightly dole cheque. Why the hell shouldn't they! The majority of litter and graffiti has been deposited by people of that ilk in the first place.

It reminds me of a story I once heard about a tramp in Montreal in Canada. One of my friends was visiting the city and saw a 'Knight of the Road', get up from his begging position, walk across the street, pick up a piece of litter, place it in a bin and return to his original resting place. It should make us ashamed of ourselves!

This, 'You owe me!' mentality has developed the, 'If there's a blame, there's a claim!' culture. What a joke this is. Whilst some claims are totally bona fide, for example victims of asbestosis or car accidents where a driver has been negligent, some just beggar belief.

I heard of a burglar who had locked himself in a garage that he was endeavouring to empty of its power tools. He was there for six days until he was released by the owner who had been on holiday. The thief took the owner to Court stating that he had been held against his will. As a result the arse-hole received £15,000 compensation.

Another 'claim' was taken up by a woman who had slipped on a wet patch in a fast food restaurant. She injured herself and was given thousands of pounds in compensation. The twist in the story is that she has created the wet patch herself. Following an argument with her boyfriend, she has thrown a medium diet Pepsi in his face.

The best one, or in my case, the one that makes my blood boil at a temperature hotter than the core of the sun, which incidentally is 27,000,000 degrees centigrade – slightly cooler than the apple inside a MacDonald's 'Hot Apple Pie', involves a woman who made international press some time ago.

She had purchased a Winnebago, a large motorised caravan, which she was driving on her own down a motorway. Travelling at 50 miles an hour, she placed the vehicle into cruise control and left the driver's seat, and entered the back of the van to make a cup of tea.

Strangely, the ten ton projectile ran off the road, overturned and was written off!!! (Written with a hint of sarcasm!) The woman claimed that the vehicle's hand book did not state that you had to remain behind the wheel when you placed the vehicle's cruise control on. She was awarded $750,000 compensation and the hand book was amended.

These examples just show how the world has turned into a complete and utter farce. One day, we will all pay the price; saying that, we already are through an increase in our insurance premiums. Actually, it is not the world that has gone mad. It is the way in which *we* manage it.

Many things irritate me beyond belief as you may have guessed from the preceding paragraphs. The lack of total common sense in this, and other westernised societies, drives me bonkers. I admit I am Victor Meldrew and Jeremy Clarkson rolled into one, and I could spout on for pages. However, for the sake of boring you, insulting just about everyone reading this, and causing myself a coronary arrest, I choose not to.

'But let me tell you this!!!'

I think all us normal, hard working, conscientious, law abiding, sensible people should create a new political party.

THE COMMON SENSE PARTY

Policies would include the right for British Airways staff to wear Christian crosses on a flight; no social security benefits to be paid to convicted terrorists; all those involved with noise pollution in social places to have their mouths sewn shut; a complete rehash of the compensation culture; anyone convicted of a serious crime to be placed on the Isle of Man until they die.

Actually this last one, if you don't mind me saying so, would be a great idea. We could shut down the prisons and remand centres, (if they are on remand, they've normally done it anyway and if they can't get bail, they are likely to do something illegal in the future or have done so in the past), at a cost saving of billions of pounds. Some of these monies would be paid to the existing residents in the Isle of Man to be relocated across Britain.

This would leave 572 square kilometres of land totally free of anyone, or anything, with more than one brain cell - an ideal place to deposit all those with no more than two. It is equidistant from Ireland, Scotland and England which is excellent as no one country would have to have sole responsibility and far enough away from any other land mass to avoid escapees.

Anyone convicted of a crime, say assault or burglary upwards, would be placed in a secure helicopter and dropped in the middle of Douglas. The Isle would be renamed 'Manky Isle' to reflect the quality of its new occupants.

Unfortunately, the famous motorcycle TT races would have to be abandoned. However, a new sports pastime could take its place. This would involve armour plated tanks and vehicles travelling along the 37.739 mile circuit, containing occupants, who have paid to shoot as much of the wild life as they can. This would save endangered wildlife in other countries, as who would want to mount the stuffed head of a baboon, when the skilled hands of a taxidermist could embalm the head of a prolific paedophile.

'Morning, Smithers! Shot a drug dealer and a gaunt white faced hoodie this morning. Mmmm – can't decide which room to hang them in.'

This would leave our green and pleasant land, green and pleasant.

I know, I know, I'm outrageous, opinionated and warped. I think I should maybe stand for MP representing one of the three main political parties.

Since writing this piece, and returning to the midst of this amble, the Daily Telegraph has continued to open up further details of our politicians' expenses. These further confirm through evidence passed to the press, that MPs are total arsehole scumbags; greedy, self centred, pedestal climbers; only interested in lining their pockets at the tax payers cost. Indeed many of them are fraudsters, who by virtue of the expenses system, a system implemented and policed by the MPs themselves, have stolen our money.

Many of the stories that have emerged from these revelations beggar belief and there is no doubt that some of the worst offenders should be hauled in front of the courts to answer charges of dishonesty. I know, I know, I have already touched on this but the revelations just continue to irritate me to distraction.

It amazes me that so many of these men and women who were elected by us, the general public, have lost all sense of what is right or wrong. They easily forget that they represent their constituencies around and about Britain and the ordinary working men and women who graft out a life for their children. As soon as they are invested into the Commons it is as though any ounce of humility and righteousness is diluted. Any criticism is thrown back in our faces. Let's not forget that these are the leaders of our country. No they aren't! They are the people who *we* elect to represent *us*.

The common threads running through the 646 representatives are threefold and depending on which MP is being questioned you will be bored rigid with the same three excuses. The first excuse in my opinion is the most worthy and is the most honest. They say,

'Let me tell you this. For many years we have felt that we are not paid a commensurate rate of pay for the responsibility of our roles and, as such, have been encouraged to use the system of expenses to 'make up' our annual remuneration package. I am sure you will all agree unequivocally, that we do a wonderful job of running this country and it is only right that we should be rewarded accordingly.'

Well possibly!

For example, the Prime Minister receives £197,869 per annum plus expenses etc. In his position, he can influence a majority led government, to go to war, to change laws, to increase or decrease taxes that we all pay. Let's face it! It is a pretty damn important position. Taking this into account, how can it be justified that the chief executive at Herts County Council, Caroline Tapster, earned a total of £202,503 in 2007/8 and what's more, she was only the 8th best paid council leader in the country. So, like it or not, they may have a point on this one. Maybe they are underpaid for the responsibilities they have, it is just a shame that they have to manipulate the system in such an underhand manner to compensate.

The second reason our beloved MPs give, is based on their self delusion that all claims are justified.

'Let me tell you this. When I claimed for two sex videos on my expenses, I did not feel that I was doing anything wrong. The system is put in place to recompense MPs for any expenses incurred in undertaking their role within the Commons. Whilst it was reported that my husband ordered the films, he did not. I rented them through Blockbusters. I had not seen my husband for a number of weeks and was becoming increasingly horny and frustrated. It was so bad that it was affecting my work on behalf of my constituents. A quick flick of my bean whilst watching 'Debbie does Dallas', has enabled me to work with additional vigour and I am totally convinced that this was a justifiable expense.'

'Why don't you just use the male underwear section of the Freemans catalogue like everyone else?'

The final reason is far more ominous and gives me significant concern for the future of our country as a whole. It is,

'Let me tell you this! When I realised that I had presented the receipt from Sexy Susie's Pleasure Emporium, I was totally distraught. This is obviously an error and should not have been claimed for. I am sorry that on this occasion I have made a mistake and I will repay the £8,459.08 immediately.'

The only mistake you have made is being caught, you tosser!!!

How many MPs have stated that they have made an error? If they can make that many errors between them, should they be in charge of our Country? Hundreds have made errors! They shouldn't be in charge of the milk monitor duties at the local primary school. And what if we had made those errors?

'Good week, George?'

'No not really Dave. I was caught fiddling my expenses. Claimed 37 second class returns to Nottingham at £48.97 and only went once!'

'Have you been sacked?'

'Oh! No! I just said sorry I'd made a mistake and offered to pay it back at 3p per annum.'

But whether it is their God given right, their ignorance or a 'mistake', it doesn't really matter. The whole issue festers in the brains of everyone in this country. We feel cheated, abused and taken for a ride. Those who have had their fingers caught in the till should be brought to justice. Anyone who has switched homes to avoid Capital Gains Tax or claimed interest on a mortgage that was repaid years ago is a fraudster.

'What I can say, is when I changed my first home to my second home four times in four years, I did this in all good faith! As you know I live in West Ealingham which is 187 yards from the Houses of Parliament. The travel was interfering with my work schedule and I therefore purchased a second home in North West Ealingham which is only 27 yards from the Commons.

'My daughter moved into my first property to set up an exclusive escort service. However, the clientele were not as discerning as here in the square mile (far more MPs you know), so after much discussion I decided to switch back. I feel it totally justified that I spent monies on the house before I left. I can honestly say that I did ensure I did not claim the whole of my £23,000 second home allowance as I was thinking of the expense to the tax payer.

'I only claimed £22,879 of allowance and this was for major alterations. I didn't want my daughter to move into a shit-house did I? Wah wah! This included the re-decoration of the boudoirs to red and gold, the changing of the beds to four posters, a dungeon with all the latest bondage gear and to site a red light over the front door. My daughter is now paying me rent of £4,800 per month and whilst I have not told the claims office of this, I do make an extra charitable donation of £5 per month to the Red Cross from my own pocket...which is then claimed back on my expenses.

'I re-iterate that I have done nothing wrong and I have only claimed allowances and expenses laid out in the guidelines. I also only made £148,000 from the sale and felt justified in changing it back to my first home to avoid CGT. By the way, did you notice I said CGT which is short for Capital Gains Tax?'

'Yes Chancellor, but who was responsible for the guidelines?'

'I can tell you this. The document that was passed to the house in a white, green , blue, yellow and brown paper, and ratified by our esteemed members, was prepared by the All Commons, All Singing All Dancing, All Profiteering, Select House of the Rising Sun Committee!'

'And who led that All Commons, All Singing All Dancing, All Profiteering, Select House of the Rising Sun Committee?'

'Let me tell you this! I did!'

There are many strange and bizarre claims that have come to light from this scandal. The claim for the cleaning of a moat was a good one; as was the duck house. And cash for lavatories. And cash for carpets. And cash for saunas. And cash for swimming pools. And cash for gardeners. And cash for barbecues. And cash for dog food. And cash for cushions; silk ones, 17 of them in all to ease the repose of Keith Vaz.

In the case of a Conservative MP with a constituency in the shires, it is cash for horse manure. One MP wants cash for Kit Kats. A Scottish Labour MP confirms the stereotype of his race by claiming 5p for a carrier bag. Well, he probably needed somewhere to stuff all his receipts. A Lib Dem takes cash for cosmetics. My favourite though was one of the earliest expenses claim to hit the papers namely: 'One male MP claims cash for tampons.'

I'm not sure whether he was a Conservative, a Socialite or a Liberal, but what is he going to do with it? Maybe he was a smoker and following the smoking ban felt that he would need a cigarette replacement whilst bartering with the lobbyists.

'I really can't decide whether to vote with or against the Government on this one and it's really making me fidgety. Where are my tampons? Do you know I've given these up so many times and I'm still going through 20 a day?'

Still it is better than at the last election when making his acceptance speech.

'Mr Returning Officer, Ladies and Gentlemen, EHHHHHHHHHHHHHHHHHHHHHHH Body Form, Body Form for uuuuuuuuuuuuuuuuuuuuuu.'

I wonder whilst going to the Commons he swims down the Thames or rides a bike. If they are Tampax he will be able to do both. If they are Lillets he has no chance. As an aside, whilst researching tampons (which is something I don't do every day), I have noticed following the usual Google search, that there is a Museum of Menstruation! Maybe the gentleman in question could seek new employment as a guide in the museum once he has been sacked at the next general election. He could also do demonstrations on how he used the fluffy cotton stick and explain how the string did not garrotte his weaner.

Shame on them all, I say-and it is nice for a change to realise that I am not alone. By the next election we are told that things will be more transparent which is a bit of a shame, for if I stand as Parliamentary Candidate for the Common Sense Party and manage to secure election victory, I won't be able to fiddle my expenses. Still, I don't use tampons and prefer Twix to Kit Kats; and there will be enough manure spoken by those who avoid the sack. Hey Ho!!

I hate driving and as far as I am concerned I just want to get where I am going as quickly as possible. I really am looking forward to the introduction of the new 20 miles per hour restrictions in built up areas. NOT! I find thirty mind blowingly boring and tedious as it is. But driving does bring out the worst in people both from an aggressive standpoint but also, on occasion, incredible selfishness.

Don't you just hate it when you are driving along a main road and there is a short gap between you and the car in front, nothing behind, and a car pulls out from a side road in the gap causing you to brake heavily? Why don't they wait until you have gone past and have the whole road to themselves? They invariably then forget to change from first to second gear and drive at 22 miles an hour.

I once knew a woman who never changed out of first gear. She changed her car from an automatic to a manual gear box and didn't realise that it didn't change itself. I also knew of one woman who would not turn right across the traffic. She always used to come to the tennis club via a route which enabled her to turn left all the way. Anyway, back to my rant.

So we now have a car in front proceeding slower than a dog with no legs and we arrive at some traffic lights which are on red. Due to the light change we have caught up with some of the traffic in front. As the lights change to green, all the first few cars pop the clutch and move away satisfactorily. But does Mr Dick For Brains in front? Oh no! He is not even aware that the lights have turned green.

When he finally looks up, he checks his mirrors, places the car into gear, lets off the hand brake, checks his mirrors again, checks his mirrors yet again and moves away at 2 miles an hour, just in case the lights change back to red. Well they do change to red; Just after Mr Dick For Brains has gone through, leaving you in a position of either having to stop or risking life and limb and three points on your licence for jumping a red light.

The other thing that really gets my goat is on the motorway. 'I like the middle lane and I'm sticking to it, Audrey. You know me, I'm a middle lane type of man, safe and careful and 58 miles an hour is an ideal speed enabling easy stopping in the event of an accident or coming across fog on this lovely sunny day.'

Well Mr Middle Lane Man! We all hate you.

The only one worse is Outside Lane Man.

'I know there is no one in the middle lane but I'm sticking to the outside lane at 68 miles an hour, as I see two slow moving lorries in the inside lane two miles in the distance.'

I have been known to overtake on the inside, a very naughty manoeuvre indeed and punishable by law. However, as Jeremy Clarkson has stated on 'Top Gear', if there is room enough on the inside lane to overtake, there is enough room for Mr Outside Lane Man to pull over and let you past. I'm not sure whether these two numpties i.e. Messrs Middle and Outside Lane Man do so to annoy, rejoice in their total selfishness or just haven't a clue that they are doing it.

I was once on a dual carriage way coming home from work. It was remarkably quiet on the stretch considering the time of day. The road went from one roundabout to another and lasted for approximately two miles. A blue Volvo estate was in the outside lane approaching the first roundabout and indicated to continue towards the second.

There were no cars in sight and the Volvo remained in the outside lane of the dual carriage way at 40 miles an hour. After ¼ of a mile I flashed him, not wanting to undertake. After ½ mile I flashed him again. He still did not move over and there were still no other cars either in front or behind.

I finally undertook him and gave him a sign as I raced through, indicating that he enjoyed rapturous sex on his own, but he continued to stare forwards and did not dare look across. You could see approximately half a mile from the next roundabout that one or two cars had built up and as I slowed down I noticed that the Volvo driver had commenced indicating to turn right at the roundabout and was flashing me like a loon to bring this matter to my attention.

This pillock of a car driver had therefore stuck in the outside lane for two miles at forty miles per hour on a duel carriageway anticipating the right turn at the roundabout. It's really not surprising that road rage is so prevalent these days and I would be lying if I didn't admit to it now and again. However, I always ensure that they are far, far smaller than me and their car has an engine size of less than 1000 cc.

Talk about road rage, I once worked with a lovely woman at a branch who was subject to an appalling and terrifying experience whilst driving with her husband. They owned an MG midget soft top car that they had lovingly restored.

One day they were driving in the country enjoying the countryside although it was not warm enough to lower the fabric roof. Approaching a roundabout, the lady's husband was in the outside lane and wished to continue straight on passing the first exit road and taking the second.

A Subaru Impreza raced up the inside lane as the husband commenced the turn. He indicated to turn off the roundabout, not seeing the boy racer and carved him up quite badly. The Subaru blasted his horn and kept his hand on it for a few seconds.

There was no damage to either car as no contact was made however, the owner of the other car was not happy at all. He followed the MG for approximately two miles down country lanes three feet away from its bumper and looking in his rear view mirror, the MG driver could see the other driver flicking V signs and clenching his fist and shouting obscenities as though he would be able to hear.

The road was in the middle of the countryside by now and was winding with no passing place. However, as soon as there was a straight the petrol head de-clutched, rammed it into second and burst past them.

Rather than accelerating away, as soon as he was passed them he slowed right down, forcing them to do the same. Within a few hundred yards he stopped forcing the MG to do the same.

He opened the driver's door and raced up to my colleague and his wife's car, walked up the front of the bonnet, all the time screaming at them. He stood on the bonnet, balanced himself on his left foot and rammed his right foot straight through the fabric roof. His foot was between the driver and the passenger and did not cause physical harm but, as you can imagine the two were scared to death.

The racer, pulled his foot up out of the car, walked back down the bonnet, got in his car and sped off. My colleague, whilst a gentle soul also was gutsy when it came to right and wrong and showing great principles took the car registration number and reported the incident to the police. The Subaru driver was arrested, charged and found guilty at a Magistrates Court and was sentenced to thirty hours community service.

It really does show to what lengths some drivers will go to, to show how annoyed they are. A truly terrifying experience and really makes you think whether it is worth entering into arguments whilst driving.

So there we have it! I must sound a very grumpy, irritable man to those who don't know me. Those who do know me would concur that I am, or certainly can be on those occasions that irritate and make me grumpy. I seem to be getting worse with age and it is probably down to the ever increasing frustration of living life. I really wish I could just draw breath and relax and let the world just pass me by without me becoming incensed at the most innocuous thing.

Bring back traditional Sundays I say, where shops are closed and the pace of life momentarily slows in anticipation of the week ahead.

Sundays used to be special days to chill, play golf or read the Sunday supplements; to visit relatives or go for a walk. The roads were always so quiet. Everybody needs time to reflect and build relationships with loved ones.

Even Tesco wasn't open. Sheer bliss!

CHAPTER TEN:

My Embarrassment Precedes Me

With history piling up so fast, almost every day is the anniversary of something awful – Joe Brainard

There are very few things I can say in life I have mastered, however, embarrassing myself in front of others, invoking cringe worthy moments and those times in life where you just want the ground to open up under your feet and bury you without a trace, or a funeral, is one.

I'm just really good at it. I haven't been to special evening classes at the local college, or studied an NVQ in 'Dickology', but I just seem to have a rare talent, an artist with free rein to spread his red faced orgy of embarrassment, wherever he goes.

An example to start you off and empower you in the belief that I am the one to trust to make you feel fidgety in my presence in case I say something I shouldn't, I recall the instance when I was representing the bank at a firm of solicitors.

This is the type of occasion I abhor and is the worst part of my current role. With strains of Obsessive Compulsive Disorder (OCD) in my blood which is triggered by certain situations, it is akin to asking someone with arachnophobia to work in the insect house at Chester Zoo. Meeting and greeting, networking and socialising with strangers bring on anxiety attacks, an agitative state and blind panic to such an extent that I have, on occasions, merely called to pick up my name badge so the host thinks I have been at the event in question and then headed for the nearest coffee shop.

I was circulating around the solicitors, however, only the ones where they were in full and frank discussion with another person I already knew. I could no way walk up to a total stranger and start talking to them. I would rather attach one of my three testicles to the National Grid.

I saw another businessman I had the misfortune to have been bored rigid by at an exact replica of the event a week earlier, talking with one senior lawyer of the firm of partners who was hosting the event. Sweating, I mingled in, hating every minute of this sordid, forced alliance. I nodded and smiled as well as anyone, maybe so well, that the great bard himself, overseeing a performance of Macbeth by the Royal Shakespeare Company, would have been overwhelmed by my inspiring rendition of the supporting role I was acting out.

The discussion between the two continued, on and on. 'Howwwws business with yoooo, Crispin?' the pompous solicitor enquired. Could I give a toss? Could I bollocks! On and on and on it went, mutual back scratching and, 'I'll show you mine if you show me yours', mentality and I was bored ridged, well, would have been if I wasn't so agitated. They shifted from business, to holidays to the size of their cars to the size of the rings on their wife's and mistress's hands. There was a sudden lull, a pause so pregnant that its waters nearly broke there and then, with the two businessmen born in Boredomsville, Tennessee, going into contraction.

"Breathe, breathe, Crispin. It will soon be over. You are nine centimetres dilated and I can see its head is engaged. Have some gas and air, I know you are full of it already but have more. It's now 10 centimetres dilated and I know you want to push. Oh! Crispin, push, push, push, harder, gas and air, push, push, I can see its head Crispin, it's coming, it's coming. Yes, yes, yes. Oh! Crispin you've given birth to the biggest bullshit I've ever seen. I'm so proud!'

The pause continued and I felt the need to interject before I fell asleep. 'Crispin, how old are your three year old twins?' I asked. The two looked at each other and back at me in total astonishment. Both turned back to look at each other, turned 180 degrees and walked off in opposite directions.

At another do of the same ilk, I remember asking one chap about his son. 'What gender is your son, Cuthbert?'

I really remind myself of Hyacinth Bouquet's next door neighbour who was always so scared to come around for a cup of tea as she knew she would break a cup; not just any cup but the finest Worcester with the hand painted periwinkles.

One cannot abate fate. Trouble is fate, in one particular area, is consistent. If it is going to happen, it will, and if it will happen to someone, it will happen to me. There is one constant in my life and that is dropping bollocks, embarrassing myself or those close to me, and I have a distinct inability to be able to engage brain before speaking.

If there is one dog turd in a twenty acre field, I would stand in it. I also wouldn't notice until I had walked into the house, up the stairs and into the bedroom. Why not spread it as far as you possibly can? It's called Murphy's Law.

A great example was when I was branch manager in one of the most affluent parts of Cheshire. The office was somewhat unusual. There was a large square banking hall, off which led doors to interview rooms. The counter was square on to the hall however, the main office was through a door on the left of the counter and one then turned left into the square office. The area behind the counter was more like a wide passage way to the stairs and first floor.

This was a good set up, as it made it virtually impossible for customers to see through to the office unless they literally leaned across the writing counter with their face up to the glass security screen, with their head cocked totally to the left. It was a great opportunity to be able to avoid those customers you wanted to avoid, for one reason or another.

The staff at that particular branch were really fun loving people and we had some great times. We were always laughing and joking. I sat in the furthest corner of four desks and there were a further two desks nearer the counter.

One particular day I received an e-mail from our area office advising that there was to be a Chinese weekend at a local stately home at which there would be demonstrations of the culture, dress, language and history of the nation. The purpose of the e-mail was to enable the managers to contact local Chinese customers and accompany them to the event, endorsing and emphasising the global nature and representation of the bank.

I read the e-mail and thoughts started to run amok. The thought of duck in Peking sauce with pancakes came to mind first and with juices developing in the saliva glands, moved my attentions to the culture of the country. I wondered what sort of events, stalls and demonstrations would be involved in the two day event. There were approximately five staff in the back office whilst I read out the e-mail in a Chinese accent.

'OOOOOOh , anywon fancy, going to Chinese weekend at Tatwon Park. OOOOOOh fwee tickets, weather good, not too cwowdy?' The staff started to laugh.

I rose from my seat and started to move my arms very slowly, pushing my fingers and hands away from my face, leaning back on my back leg supporting my weight. I moved my weight onto my front leg and lifted my back leg up in slow motion. The staff started to really laugh.

'OOOOOOOH,' emitted from the back of my throat, as I emulated the 800 year old lineage form of Chang San Feng, the 13th century founder of Tai Chi. I wanted to develop enlightenment and skills for entering the Supreme Mystery, often translated as 'Primordial Qigong' or 'Primordial Tai Chi'. Qigong is the historical Mother of Tai Chi done for health and spiritual development, and is much older than Tai Chi done for martial self-defence and I was fully versed in each and every aspect of this ancient art.

I was in a trance-like state. With smooth, slow motions, I painted pictures with my sublime body and limbs. Deep within myself and oblivious of everything around me, I was engulfed in peace and tranquillity.

The staff, by now, were guffawing and even though I was in a deep inner trance, a small tear fell down my cheek, like a Lotus flower petal falling in all its beauty. I once again moved my body in perfect harmony, forming another shape, feeling deeper and deeper at one with my soul and the effervescence of nature's appeal. The air was suddenly filled with a haunting silence, not a wisp of a sound cut the air. I opened my eyes but continued my meditation. I observed that in the world outside my body, the other life forms were no longer smiling but appeared tense and out of spirits with their souls.

'Steve, Steve, stop it!'

'OOOOOOOOH, I am in-gwashiated in my inner beeeing.'

'Steve, for God's sake! Stop it!!!' The voice had some urgency and brought me out of the trance which had captivated me.

My colleague's neck twitched and I realised that she was attempting to bring something at the counter to my attention. I turned my head and looked across. To my horror, my only Chinese customer had his head right up to the counter glass, head cocked, and had witnessed every action and exclamation I had made. I quickly sat down.

The stunning hues of deepened, crimson red, forced across the sky, as the sun and horizon infused across Africa's Sarrengetti, were nothing compared to the cheeks of the bank manager's face in Cheshire.

I worried for the next week that I would be hauled up in front of my area manager following a head office complaint. However, and luckily for me, this was not forthcoming and I am grateful to the customer who must of had a profound sense of humour, or thought that I was proficient in the art of Tai Chi. Should he ever wish to learn some of my moves to find radiant enlightenment within his innermost sanctum, I would be only too pleased to share.

I enjoyed some great friendships at that particular branch and we always were playing tricks on each other and generally had good times. One of the workers there was called Mary Wilson, not the black lady in the Supremes, but just as personable. On one day, I went into work and had been going through the usual drudgery with a happy heart, knowing that I was representing the bank that afternoon at a corporate golf day at Davenport Golf Club.

I was enjoying a moment of light relief with Mary and a few others and I opened a Peppermint Aero chocolate bar. With mouth awash with saliva, I slipped the whole bar out of the green wrapper and took off the green silver foil that surrounded the rectangle of sweet delight. Boy was I looking forward to munching my way through it.

'Are you going to give me some squares?' enquired Mary, obviously infatuated with the confectionery as much as I was. I didn't answer but instead, stuffed the whole of the bar into my mouth at once, ensuring that my gluttony was satiated and generosity avoided.

The bar was made by the chocolatier, to be consumed in bite sized chunks and whilst my mouth on occasion appears large when measured in decibels, volumetrically I would say it was relatively average. The milk chocolate coating and green bubble infused centre, filled the gaping orifice to its limits, stretching the boundaries of the surface area to their maximum. I was not able to bite or chew the offending article as there was nowhere for it to go, other than outwards or downwards. The confection was intransient other than the small trickle of melted nectar that was dribbling down the back of my throat.

Then the worst possible thing that could happen, did happen. Mary began to laugh. I couldn't move my mouth, however, I was able to move my eyes and saw out of its corners that she was giggling uncontrollably. I began to laugh, not outwardly but within myself, tears forming, ducts streaming, stomach locking, no exit, no way out.

Rather than the green chocolate mass forcing through the locked jaws, the back wash of melted mintyness shot upward, directed from the back of the roof of the mouth pallet. It passed the pharynx, into the nasal cavity, the maxilla and ethmoid bones ensuring the stream of tasty green, shot through the ostia, down through the mucus membrane, and out of the nostrils creating a two lane motorway of sticky brown and lime sweetness from my top lip to the bottom of my chin.

I remember to this day, all afternoon on the golf course, attempting to represent the bank to the best of my ability, having to constantly blow my nose. Not only did I have to contend with the colour and composition of the edible mucus but also the smell of peppermint on every breath. I have not purchased from the purveyor of chocolate a similar product since.

I once read a great story in one of those lady's magazines that are so bland in content and appearance, and follow a template layout proforma of utter drivel and inconsequence. They always follow the same pattern; Fashion for the masses, relationships, soft furnishings, food recipes, true stories, for example,' I married my sister's milkman', adverts for breast enlargement, and a short story. However, in this particular publication each week, was a reader's 'most embarrassing moment'.

It told the tale of a young woman who was on a first date with a dishy man whom she really wanted to impress. The story was only a couple of paragraphs long, so I could use artistic licence and embellish it. However, for the sake of the environment in which we live, global warming etc., I will keep it brief.

The date comprised of a taxi ride to a very exclusive and expensive Italian restaurant, a gourmet meal, to be followed by possibly the best sex she had or may ever experience. She was out to impress and had dressed appropriately.

She ordered Pasta Marinara described as tender spaghetti strands, blanketed in a zesty fresh-tasting marinara sauce that gets its kick from capers and red pepper flakes. It didn't say what he ordered, but I presume that he avoided the ribs or the Spaghetti Bolognese which one should never eat on a first date. Maybe he ordered the oysters, hoping his luck would be in.

He was a hunk and she was smitten. She hung on every word he said. He was romantic, manly, yet gentle, infused with passion. He showed humility and understanding but most of all, he had a fantastic sense of humour. Our girl was in love at first sight and wanted to see him again, certainly on an occasion with slightly less attire and in a place not so crowded. She laughed and laughed and stared into his adoring, deepest, blue eyes. She laughed and laughed and disaster struck.

One of his throw away, humorous quips was really funny. Not only finding it hilarious, but also on a high from the expensive wines and heady atmosphere of the mating, she guffawed with gusto. What she neglected to recognise was that she had just taken a large mouthful of freshly made spaghetti and her body was not able to cope with so many senses at once.

She began to choke violently to such a degree that he stood up out of his chair. It was his intention to attempt the Heimlich manoeuvre later back at his flat, with her bent over the bed and not to thrust his fist and thumb into her abdomen, it involving other organs and effect. However, he was prepared to undertake Mr Heimlich's manoeuvre to save the day. It was not needed, however.

Suddenly she re-gained composure, took a drink of wine and apologised for the outburst. He sat down and just stared at her. Dangling from her nose was a four inch piece of spaghetti which rocked from side to side in tandem with the airflow to the nearest air conditioning unit. She immediately noticed that there must be something wrong and felt something cold touch her chin and stick to it. She lifted her arm up and with index finger and thumb pinched the end of the spaghetti strand and pulled it away from her face. As she pulled, the four inches became, five, became, six, became seven, finally dropping the previously embalmed end, back onto the middle of the bowl from where it originally came. An embarrassing moment indeed!

It never went on to say whether they met again or the Heimlich manoeuvre was performed later that evening but I am sure that she will never eat in an Italian restaurant again and certainly won't order spaghetti on a first date.

In the section in the same magazine the following week was a fairly similar story but occurred at a party where a single woman was attracted to a single man. They had commenced cognitive rutting therapy. They were attracted to each other and were flirting without conscience. They both had drinks and she lifted her free arm up to the mantelpiece, set high above the fire place and her eye-line, to reach for some salted peanuts in a bowl. Taking a handful of nuts, she giggled in an evocative manner at a smutty throw-away one-liner emitted from the lips of the new found friend. She cupped her hand to contain the nuts and threw them into her mouth in one.

She immediately realised that she had tossed not peanuts into her mouth, but seven Benson and Hedges cigarette butts. I bet he didn't fancy kissing her that evening. "Bugger me! She smelt like an old ashtray!"

Whilst I am on the subject of humiliating experiences which have occurred to others rather than me, I recall a number of stories which had been submitted by readers of one of the widest read men's magazine; not the top shelf variety I must point out, albeit, I gather that some of the more straight laced newsagents are placing them in brown paper on that shelf. No! One of those that are supposed to be the equivalent of the more trendy and raunchy women's mags, containing articles that would appeal to men: Football, Naked women, Booze, Accidents, Naked women, Cars, Naked Women, etc.

One of those stories concerned a reader who had wooed a mate for rutting at a local bar. (For those of you old enough who would remember Terry Thomas, 'Saddle that filly,' and, 'Are you ready? Are you ready nowwww?' prior to his game of tennis, springs to mind). I've always loved the word woo. 'I wood her and then gave her one in the back alley', just doesn't sit right does it?

Anyway, the young stag, chatted the flirtatious doe up all night and they became more and more amorous. At kicking out time, they had been playing the delights of tonsil tennis and both felt that they wished to take the matter a little further. As he lived with his mother, they agreed to go back to her flat which was just around the corner from the bar that they had met in, and they walked in a fairly unsteady gait to her front door. He kissed her again on the door step and she opened the door and they walked in. She poured a couple of red wines in the kitchen and sat down close to him on the sofa.

The petting continued apace and soon they were both highly aroused, their bestial passions heightened, and down to their underwear.

'Just give me a couple of minutes,' she breathlessly murmured, and disappeared to the toilet. He sat there in an anticipative state, awaiting her return.

'Shit, I didn't shower this morning!' he thought. Rising, (in more ways than one), he stood up and walked into the kitchen. Not flicking the light switch, he walked up to the sink and reached for the dishcloth. Pulling away the front of his underpants, he quickly freshened his manhood and its pubic surround, threw the dishcloth back onto the drainer and returned to his seated position on the sofa just as she returned.

The petting commenced and was unabated. She started to kiss him on his chest and she dropped to her knees her lips, licking, lowering, and searching for the rod of iron beneath his briefs. He lay back in ecstasy as her journey of wantonness continued. She passed his belly button and continued down kissing, licking, sucking, biting his skin reaching her goal, knowing that she too would reach the zenith of satisfaction in due course. (I'm enjoying writing this and will maybe have to write a naughty novel next!)

'What the hell is this?'

He knew something was seriously wrong instantly. He lifted his head up far enough for him to see her face just above the sofa cushions. Only her head was visible from his position but he realised that it was serious from her expression. In slow motion her hand appeared above the sofa holding a small oval object.

'What the fuck is a Heinz baked bean doing in your pubes?'

Such stories are probably less rare than you think. Whilst happenings occur which invoke a high state of embarrassment to me, often, they also appear to affect others. Yet it does always seem to be a small cross section of people, a small percentage of the population that it affects, more than the majority. I think it might be a faulty gene, handed down through generations, which is debilitating and the cause of many a red face. The thing is, the majority of the situations could be avoided and it is normally just a question of engaging one's brain before either speaking, or completing an action.

In another of the men's mag articles was the story of a chap and his mate going to a football match where his team was playing away from home. He had driven and he and the friend were desperately looking for a car parking space on a side road adjoining the ground. They had been searching for some time, kick off loomed, and they feared missing the beginning of the match. They were both becoming somewhat frustrated and irritated at their lack of luck and they turned into another street where a row of cars were parked nose to tail on both sides.

As they turned, at the opposite end, approximately two hundred yards in front of them, was a police car coming towards them. The road was wide and plenty of room for the cars to pass without difficulty.

As the vehicles drew closer and closer, the football fan looked at the driver of the police car. He was a traffic cop, driving a liveried, top spec Volvo and as he approached he was looking sternly at him. Suddenly the police man lifted his right hand placing his thumb and fingers into a circle akin to an opened fist.

He moved his hand up and down staring at the other driver as he came nearer. The fan was aggrieved to say the least. Whether it was the fact that they were away supporters and were sporting coloured scarves out of the driver and passenger windows, was no reason for a man of law to make such a gesture inferring that the chap enjoyed the delights of sexual DIY rather more than he should, even if he did support the home team.

The driver in his anger, lifted his right hand, made a V sign, and frantically pumped his hand up and down, moving it in an arced crescent, following the policeman's outraged glare, as the police car moved passed. The fan reached the end of the street and had to stop for traffic and he looked in his rear view mirror. The Volvo's brake lights were lit, as were the reversing lights, as was the 'STOP POLICE' sign. A short blast of police alarm whooped the air and the vehicle reversed so that both drivers were face to face, divided by the two panes of glass. The policeman stepped out of his patrol car.

'Step out of the car, please Sir!' The footie fan opened the door and pulled himself out of the car feeling rather irate albeit somewhat fearful of the repercussions of his actions.

'Please could you tell me why you have just gesticulated in such an offensive manner to an Officer of the Law?'

'I told you to fuck off because you were calling me a wanker!'

'I wasn't calling you 'a wanker', Sir, I was telling you to put your seat belt on.'

What a complete classic. I could have been this fan, this fan could have been me; upon reflection, I don't think I could ever call, or gesticulate to a policeman in such a manner. I would have liked to on a number of occasions and have behind their backs but not in such a forthright and obvious way.

Murphy's Law has always been part of my life and one which I respect and accept the consequences at all times. According to the American Dialect Society, member Stephen Goranson found a version of the law, not yet generalized or bearing that name, in a report by Alfred Holt at an 1877 meeting of an engineering society:

'It is found that anything that can go wrong at sea generally does go wrong sooner or later, so it is not to be wondered that owners prefer the safe to the scientific.... Sufficient stress can hardly be laid on the advantages of simplicity. The human factor cannot be safely neglected in planning machinery. If attention is to be obtained, the engine must be such that the engineer will be disposed to attend to it.'

American Dialect Society member Bill Mullins found a slightly broader version of the aphorism in reference to stage magic. The British stage magician Nevil

Maskelyne wrote in 1908, 'It is an experience common to all men to find that, on any special occasion, such as the production of a magical effect for the first time in public, everything that *can* go wrong *will* go wrong. Whether we must attribute this to the malignity of matter or to the total depravity of inanimate things, whether the exciting cause is hurry, worry, or what not, the fact remains.'

Murphy's law emerged in its modern form no later than 1952, as an epigraph to a mountaineering book by Jack Sack, who described it as an 'ancient mountaineering adage.'

'Anything that can possibly go wrong, does.'

Well you now know the history of Murphy's Law and I am glad that my book is enhancing your intellect and knowledge of all things important. To enforce this new found comprehension and awareness of this debilitating cancer that affects those unlucky enough to suffer from it, I conclude with further examples which have happened to me.

Ten or eleven years ago, I was lying in a reclining chair on the patio at our old house in Cheadle Hulme, Cheshire. It was a glorious summer's day, one of those that we do not seem to enjoy often enough. I had cut the lawn and the heady aroma of fresh sliced grass filled the humid air. A gentle breeze drifted across the adjoining bowling green and rustled through the trees. There were no sounds, other than the birds singing with joy at the beauty of the day, and the distant knocking of bowls as the bowlers battled for the jack.

I was basking in the sun, close to the house, lying, enchanted by the warmth of the rays, drifting in semi-consciousness, feeling the whispering wind caress my naked body, enjoying the relaxation and tranquillity of the moment.

It all happened in a split second.

BANG - an explosion within three feet of my head. Instantaneously a warm object landed on my sun kissed stomach, followed by an unearthly scratching feeling of an alien attempting to burrow its way into my body. It all happened so quickly and with such force that I was shocked into panic. Heart pumping blood through my body making the veins expand to breaking point, I launched my invaded body out of the reclining chair and up onto my feet.

The demon that had tried to enter me, fell from my lap and I jumped backwards. The recliner was the perfect height to increase the trauma and scythed the back of my knees. Balance was lost and my torso retreated at a gathering pace, falling backwards across the chair. Only when my body hit the floor did my legs release and I completed a backwards roll. Olga Korbut in the 1972 Olympic Games captivated the Munich audience and millions on the television with a routine slightly less dynamic, physical and well orchestrated.

I lay on the ground and, anaesthetised from the pain by adrenalin pumping through my battered body, opened my eyes to see what foreign being had caused this dramatic change in state of harmony with life.

Lying four feet away from me in a prostrate position was a large blackbird, wings spread, its feathers fanned, totally black other than its yellow beak and eye ring from which a charcoal eye peered at me, appearing as startled as its foe. I could see from the look in its eye that he knew that we had both been affected by this strange affinity and introduced by Mr Murphy.

Dazed and confused by the kamikaze attack on the Pilkington double glazed window adjacent to the chair, it slowly stood, shook its battered head, rustled its wings and took flight with the grace and beauty that it has initially arrived. To this day, I still believe that it turned its head shortly after take-off, nodding as if to say, 'Maybe we will meet again, somewhere, sometime, some place.' Either that or, 'Thanks for breaking my fall, you saved my life!' (What a load of rubbish I write sometimes.)

It's that old chestnut though, isn't it? What are the chances of a blackbird, flying into a window? Well it does happen every day somewhere in the world. Yet, what are the chances of it falling on to a half naked, half asleep human body, who ends up more damaged than the fallen bird itself? Bizarre!

The next story not only emphasises Murphy's ability to affect all and sundry, including potential relationships, but also how he can make one feel terribly uneasy about oneself, embarrassed and disconcerted. It also emphasises how close those of us sometimes sail close to the wind, in attempting to make our fellow humans laugh and why, on occasion, we wished we weren't the funny one in the gang and just listened to others, awaiting them to stumble and fall into the abyss of self-destruction into which we often drop.

Rosa, Daniel and I were on a skiing holiday in Les Coches in the French Alps. We were staying in a catered chalet which means that the party was looked after by a chalet host who undertook the cooking and cleaning etc. Whilst our party consisted of the three of us, the chalet held fifteen, and twelve other guests were shortly to arrive from all over the country, mainly from the South, via the Gatwick flight. It was fairly late on by the time they landed and upon delivery to the chalet, all children went to bed, whilst the adults introduced themselves, as we were all to be living out of each other's pockets for the next seven days.

None of the adults knew each other, other than their own partners of course however, there seemed some real characters amongst the group, which boded well for the rest of the holiday. Although most had only just arrived, all were very happy to stay up drinking the free champagne and wine that was provided by our generous host.

The wine flowed and flowed and even though we had just met them we were having a great time. At this time in my life, I was a real joker and had a host of gags for a host of subjects and I commenced my story and joke telling as though we had all known each other for many years. We were all crying, and others were interjecting, telling jokes of their own.

Tears of laughter were flowing well into the night and I started to tell a joke which had recently been the subject of Terry Wogan's mirth and delight on his breakfast show. Although Terry didn't tell the gag over the air as it was not suitable for the discerning early morning listeners, he often referred to the punch line and it was a joke that obviously he and his fellow presenters and producer were familiar.

It concerned two gentlemen, very hard of hearing, visiting a hostelry which they had not frequented before. One sat down at a table and the other went to the bar. The gentleman at the bar waited his turn and when the bartender was free he asked for two pints of bitter. 'That will be five pounds thirty, please,' stated the barman.

' Five pwonds thirty! Thaaats werry expensive,' stated the man, hard of hearing.

'It is expensive however, we have to cover the cost of the live entertainment on tonight. We have a band on!'

'Oh, live muusic, I luv liive muusic. Whaat is it? Is it skiffle?' suggested the man sounding a little like Stephen Hawking, the British theoretical physicist.

'No! It's not skiffle,' responded the barman.

'It is wock and woll?' enquired the man hard of hearing.

'No it's not rock and roll,' replied the bartender, 'It's Country and Western.'

By this time the whole party bar two, were crying with laughter at my accent which totally humiliated any human afflicted by this debilitating condition. I was dribbling down my chin as I was trying to emulate the deaf chap attempting to speak. Back to the story....

The deaf chap returned to his friend with the pints of frothing beer.

'Its werry expensive but thevve got a band on,' stated the man, hard of hearing.

'Ooh, liive muusic, I luv liive muusic. Whaat is it? Is it skiffle?' suggested the other man who also sounded a little like Stephen Hawking's twin brother, the other British theoretical physicist.

'No! It's noo skiffle,' responded his friend.

'It is wock and woll?' enquired the man.

'No it's not wock and woll,' replied the other man,

'It's some Cunt from Preston.'

The whole place erupted with guffawing, drunken, future downhillers, other than a man and wife who were not laughing at all. They made excuses and a hasty retreat to their beds. We carried on for a while, and then departed to our various rooms, looking forward to the following day and a cracking skiing fun fest.

The next morning, we were all a little worse for wear, and arrived at the breakfast table in dribs and drabs. I shuffled into a chair against the wall and Rosa and Daniel sat opposite me. A full cooked English breakfast was presented to us and we commenced the butchery of its meaty contents with gusto.

The couple who were first to leave the night before, were last to arrive to breakfast and accompanying them were their children, two girls aged around six and eight and a small boy, aged probably three. The spectacled boy was wearing two hearing aids, one in each ear.

My final story on the subject was another out of a men's magazine. It concerned a man who was driving his car through a country village heading into town. It was a really hot day and unfortunately the young chap in his twenties did not have air conditioning. As a result, he had his driver's side window full open to let in as much cool ram air as possible.

As he drove casually along he saw in the distance approximately three hundred yards in front of him was a lorry and beyond that, traffic lights which were on green. He realised that he would not reach the lights in time to go through and therefore coasted up to the lorry.

At the traffic lights were two lanes, one to go straight on and another to turn right. The lorry had chosen to go right whilst our intrepid explorer the left lane. Both drew to a stop as the lights turned red.

The car driver looked across at the vehicle besides him. It was a cattle lorry full of prime beef stock on two tiers with approximately fifty Aberdeen Angus on board, presumably just purchased from the agricultural market in the village he had just passed.

Enjoying the warmth of the sunlight albeit slightly hot due to the lack of cool air, he sat there patiently, humming along to the radio, his arm resting on the window opening.

Suddenly, a stream of warm fluid hit him flush on the cheek spraying in every direction, a small rainbow created as the liquid spray blocked out the sun. The driver's arm automatically came up to shield his face from the liquid, however, it continued for what seemed like minutes.

It finally stopped and the driver, totally soaked, pulled his arm away from the window and looked for the source of the hosing. Just as he looked across at the truck a cow's tail was descending to its normal position.

He could see through the wooden lats of the lorry the cow with his back to him. The animal had lifted its tail and fired piss straight through the gap.

Now that is unlucky and puts my blackbird saga into very much second position in the Murphy's Law league table.

CHAPTER ELEVEN:

Depression, OCD, Anxiety and My Black Dog

No one can make you feel inferior without your consent – Eleanor Roosevelt

...my grief was too deeply rooted to be cured by words – Orinda

Memories like olives, are an acquired taste – Max Beergohm

The cold cadaver lay on the unmade bed staring into a void. The body was not resting in the normal 'at peace' position but lay in recovery, one dead knee bent over the top of the other, one dead arm over the other, its left shoulder pointing towards the light. Its head was motionless and had long since functioned.

To the side of the bed was a window through which the body peered out. Thick steel bars, icy cold, ran from top to bottom every six inches, partially barring the view. Whilst imprisoning, the window was stunningly beautiful. Sun beams radiated a fusion of crimson, orange and gold refracted by the glass and exploded into the room casting an illumination of dancing flowers on the room's walls. Colours embraced and merged, forming new shades and hues incandescence so beautiful, only to dissipate and part, seeking out others rays with which to blend. For this window offered a gateway to another place far beyond the imagination of the man that looked towards it.

For the living it was possible to touch the other world through the bars and many who were agile and headstrong enough had achieved this goal. However, the beating, stifling summer sun forcing through the fortified window could not penetrate or radiate into the mind of the dead.

The man's body was not damaged in any visible way. No blood seeped through gaping wounds. No bruises blackened his pale body. All bones, muscles and organs were intact and would have functioned perfectly well had their possessor had the governance to control them. The body had not died from any cranial malfunction and the spine would have carried him perfectly well if it had the mind to. Yet the man was dead.

The bluey-grey eyes stared forward. Reflections of the other world danced and darted across the moisture that remained on his glazed pupils, forming patterns and shapes that the cadaver had not seen whilst he was alive. The shapes had always been available to view, however, one had to have the ability to see through the window to fully understand and appreciate them. The cadaver had never been able to see through the window as he had never seen the window itself. He had only ever managed to see the blackened bars that contained him.

The shapes contained wondrous beauty, where every change in its makeup presented a new vision of utopia. They presented a world of purpose and promise, where each miniscule fragment was a place to be astonished, awestruck, overcome with the simplicity, yet exquisite nature, of the piece. The pieces were individual and unique, bespoke in their purpose, however, they were all indefinably linked and every tiny fragment, each wondrous in itself, interwoven to present an awesome whole.

A bead of perspiration metamorphosed from the cadaver's forehead, seeking the easiest route for release. Weighted by gravity, it gathered pace creating a tiny stream over the wrinkle lines, plunging onwards over the bridge of his nose and into the right eye. The eye did not blink as it was transfixed by the black icy bars of the window.

As time went by, the sun's phosphorescent beams started to wane and the light began to fade. Whilst radiance continued to cascade through the window, it was less dramatic, less dynamic in its effect and as the star disappeared behind the horizon, an all consuming darkness fell on the window. The window was backlit from the rays of the quarter moon battling to show itself from behind the forming clouds, which billowed up and infiltrated the night sky. The window was visible no more.

The bars formed a charcoal gate, a silhouetted portcullis. This gate was not pearl white and, whilst in the clouds, was not guarded by Saint Peter, the keeper of the keys to the kingdom of heaven. A visitor to these gates awaited judgement and those not fit to enter heaven were denied entrance at the gates, thus descending into hell. This gate was the entrance to the Devil's abode itself and could only be opened in the darkness that ensued. The cadaver awaited an invitation to open the gate and meet his affiliation.

In a fragment of the moment, the cadaver's eyes shut tight and the man drifted into a troubled sleep.

The cold cadaver lay on the unmade bed staring into a void...........

I wrote that piece and showed it to Rosa, who did not understand where it would fit into my book. However, if you read 'between the lines' so to speak, it does represent how depressives see our world. Withdrawn, isolated and remote; removed and secluded are all adjectives which readily spring to mind.

How deep, dark and lonely is one's mind if you allow it, or to be more specific, how it wishes to control you. One who is susceptible to depression has little power over the brain's ability to control it in a rational and balanced way. In the depths of despair, I have always felt like it is an out of body experience, with the body just providing the generator, the working machine, a shell.

Whilst an outer force which is the brain, albeit, within this living breathing body takes control it is almost as though you can see yourself from the outside, but cannot control your emotions and feelings and have no inclination, will, or determination to do so.

One's eyes see things, however the brain does not interpret what it sees in a reasonable manner. An event, or emotion gleaned from an occurrence, may appear normal within one's own mind, but it is the way in which that event or emotion is interpreted and portrayed to others that determines whether one's mind is balanced or not. However, it is only to others who either know you well, or are professionally trained, who can identify that something is not right, particularly in the early stages of depression.

Often problems with your depression manifest themselves to those who even don't know you, and can be seen in the shell one calls, 'one's body'. When you are truly depressed, you really couldn't give a shit what anybody else thinks about you. Why should you think what anyone else thinks, when you couldn't give a toss about yourself?

Often you loathe yourself! Depression is the most selfish illness of them all. Everything you think about and are concerned about is oneself. This isn't selfishness. This is the illness and your inability to help yourself.

One cannot address this and the more a person feels down, the less it matters what others think. When one has suicidal intrusive thoughts, it is not at the forefront of your mind to notice whether you had a shave that morning or changed your underpants.

'Pull yourself together!' to a sufferer of depressive tendencies means,

'You need to look more deeply at yourself as you are not normal.'

To a depressive, 'Look on the bright side of life,' means little, as there is no bright side of life. There is just the dark side, and the black side.

For years and years, I have awoken every morning, and in my mind sighed and my heart has lowered, for I have to survive yet another day. I have to stay wake for another sixteen hours and do things I gain no pleasure from whatsoever. Nothing makes this better.

Yes! There is respite. On a golfing holiday with one's mates, the nadir is raised up the scale. Part, or even on occasion, most of the day, one appears to be enjoying, however deep down you are only enduring. I always feel that these moments are pauses, neither to be fully enjoyed or despised. Depressed people survive. They do not gain pleasure from occurrences and happenings that 'normal' people enjoy. Life is a chore, to be endured, minute by minute, hour by hour, and day by day.

As one drops into the abyss of despair, it is harder and harder to pull oneself up and out. It is virtually impossible to do this without professional help advice and medication. Nothing matters; Nothing whatsoever! Weariness, self loathing and no self esteem, a total lack of motivation are all traits of this, I have found in my battle against this appalling affliction.

One would rather sit in a chair for ten hours and stare at the clock, look out of a window, sleep, or curl up in a ball than to do anything physical or, in fact, anything at all.

Oneself, and one's lack of worth, is all consuming and you have not the inclination, motivation, or will to do anything about it. It is the blackest, darkest place and is infinite in depth. Once one is falling, one doesn't open the parachute to slow the fall, but point straight down hands pointed, arms outstretched, as streamline as possible, to go faster, as that is the only way you want to go. The lower is the better, as one can curl up into a smaller and smaller ball, hoping that one day the ball will become so small it no longer exists. For those that fall too far, it doesn't.

Going back to the selfish side, how can one truly love, cherish and be devoted to others, when you cannot even like or love yourself. You try your best to be as loving and as caring as possible; however, this is often viewed in a different way by the recipient, compared to receiving this attention from one with a balanced mind.

Depression is the most tiring affliction of the lot in my eyes. Try sitting on a chair and do nothing for ten hours and it's amazing how knackered you feel. It is also the loneliest of all afflictions. No-one can help. How can anyone else help if you don't want to even help yourself? It is purgatory on earth and I do believe that in some religions earth is deemed as such.

Maybe they are right? It's the old adage used elsewhere in this book, 'Is the cup half full or half empty?' I have often deemed that life is purgatory as mentioned in the Bible. If there is a God, how could he allow such misery, war, famine and destruction to something he himself created? It would be like building yourself a palatial home and then knocking it down, brick by brick.

My own religion consists of a wild belief that we are in a holding bay, from birth to death, awaiting something much worse or much better.

My Goodness! I am in a depressed mood today and think that I should turn my writing skills to something more cheery.

Self harming! This is an interesting concept and thankfully I have only done this on three occasions, one from feeling very vulnerable and the other two emanated from anxiety attacks, developing into a high state of agitation.

In this agitated state, in my case, it always starts with my legs bouncing or rocking, then hand wringing, then scratching my nail against my hand, or tapping the back of my hand on my face. It is amazing when you look at body language, how these concepts manifest on a fairly regular basis in everyday life.

Next time you are at a job interview or waiting for an appointment at the dentist, look at people waiting in the queue. Everyone can experience, and probably has at some time or other, this state of mind, however, it is to what degree, and how you can control its cause and effect, that determines the outcome and in particular the damage.

One can scratch a thumb nail over the opposite hand hard a number of times, and nothing happens. Do it two hundred times before you realise you are doing it, or indeed do it two hundred times because you want to do it, is another matter. Some say it is to draw attention – 'a cry for help', or uncontrollable frustration at a certain situation.

On other occasions it is self retribution for one's own loathing. You want to hurt yourself because you hate yourself and deserve it. All I can say is that it is a very scary place to be and I hope you never reach that black place.

The saddest thing is that this self abuse is so prevalent amongst young people, particularly teenage girls. I despair that children are so unhappy in their young lives that they feel a need to do this. It fills me with great sorrow. On many occasions it is due to peer pressure or bullying and my heart goes out to each and every one of them.

The other time I self harmed was when I was being bullied at school. I used to cut an old lady's lawn next door for 50p. I got it in my head that if I scratched my face it would make me look a little tougher at school, or, if I scratched my face the usual bullies would leave me alone the next day, as it was quite obvious that I had already been injured by something or someone.

I therefore purposely walked into a tree branch with my face. Odd, I know but I am odd and that is why I don't have many friends, as I have scared them all away! I wanted a scar to look like action man, tough and strong, 'No bastard is going to kick sand in my face! No! I'm so hard that I can walk into a cherry blossom and end up like 007.' A cry for help me thinks!!

I have suffered from Obsessive Compulsive Disorder (OCD) for many years. Whenever paying for something in cash in Greggs the bakery, I always have to place each coin dispensed head side up. If ever we are playing heads or tails, always go tails and you will always win!! I always seem to lose everything I do so play for big money!!

This is a very mild form and has affected many people from cleaning to turning the gas off, to going out and going in. My worst case was the old 'noisy neighbour syndrome'.

When I lived at my previous address in the nineties, we had a neighbour opposite who was quite happy to go away for the weekend and leave his three thugs to babysit the house. Whilst one was old enough to look after the other two, their immaturity led to fairly dramatic problems on a number of occasions.

We were lucky to live in a lovely residential road and the house in question was directly opposite, a large five bedroomed detached which had been adapted for a wheelchair, albeit, the family's only disablement was a complete lack of braincells. (And they were ginger!!!)

On one such occasion, the first I knew about a party was when six or seven yobbos ran across my front lawn. These were school chums of the eldest boy and all attended a very posh grammar school, Stockport Grammar to be exact. Who says that the posh can't be as insensitive, uncaring and crass as those born into less humble abodes?

The music was loud and in time gangs from the local council estate turned up, obviously hearing that the party was on from some irresponsible attendees down at the local off-licence. It soon was totally out of hand and the police were called by my next door neighbour who was a Deputy Police Commissioner and decided enough was enough when he saw three lads urinating on his car.

That night, I experienced a dreadful panic attack and basically drank myself into oblivion.

Approximately, three weeks later the same thing happened, albeit the parents had asked a relative to sit in the house. However, he was left cowering in a back room by the time the police were called a second time.

My OCD was borne, well and truly. I hated Saturday nights and would always either want to go out until as late as possible, or alternatively have friends around for a meal, in order that I would have 'back up' should anything un-towards happen.

I would look out of the window up to forty times a night to see if there were any parties going on down the road. If there was any other car, other than the occupant's car of certain houses, this would bring on a massive panic attack comprising shortness of breath, increased heart rate, feeling sick, feeling sweaty, shaking with fear and I just wanted to curl up in a small ball and cry myself to sleep.

This, I know, was totally irrational, however I just could not help it. To this day, I am convinced that noise, groups and parties trigger the images and feelings of when I was a child, lying in bed scared shitless about going in to school the next morning.

The drug Seroxat, so badly covered in the press was prescribed and I found the drug superb in combating these fears. I was once speaking to a representative of Smith Kline Beecham who produced the product about the suicide rate amongst the users of this drug. Her pitch was that the drug was so good that it made people well enough to gain the strength to actually do something with their miserable existence i.e. give them the will to commit suicide. Whether that or the sceptic's view is true, I know it worked for me. The curtains rarely twitched after a few weeks.

However, the same feelings manifest themselves on a fairly regular basis these days, but lean more towards my going out. I still have panic attacks when going to concerts, pubs and restaurants and the easiest thing to do is not to go. This of course has rather sad implications for the family who miss out.

At the Priory, I was having treatment in this respect which encouraged me to face my fears and put myself in those situations which make me feel most uncomfortable. This cognative therapy is based on attempting to change how your brain assesses the flight or fight scenario and endeavours to literally change the way you think.

Unfortunately, my BUPA funding has run out and at £120 a pop it is rather expensive to self fund. I just need to get out and do it. Alas, it is harder than you think when you are not a balanced, stabalised, rational human being as you are, my learned reader.

So, what a complete a fucking miserable chapter this has become, however it is a staple part of the Sheardie diet of life which has been my dogma for the last ten years. I do not expect anyone to understand. I could never understand any of these conditions myself earlier on in life. Depression, OCD, anxiety attacks and self harm are all illnesses that the majority of the population will never truly experience. However, there is an advert on the television at the moment which I find most pertinent and truly comforting.

Ruby Wax, the comedienne and TV personality states that one person in five will suffer from dandruff in their lives and one person in four will suffer from depression. She goes on to say that she suffers from both.

I cannot list every self help book, organisation, web site etc. However, if you gain nothing from these 70,000 words of total drivel, please believe me! Help, and good constructive help, is available for every one of the afflictions I have experienced and covered in my uneducated dictat.

I am not a psychiatrist, I'm a bank manager, and I really know sod all, other than the fact that I have suffered badly from each and every one of them. I also know that very few people understand what you are going through but you are not alone. On the proviso that I have not topped myself before finishing this epilogue, I can fully recommend seeking help and more important, as quickly as possible.

IT'S AN ILLNESS, NOT A WEAKNESS! DO SOMETHING ABOUT IT!

Now just to conclude this very sad section I just want to present to you another of my parodies. No doubt this will really make you feel like topping yourselves too and maybe we could have a Moony type poison fest, each sipping from the cup in turn, only to fall dead at the foot of our maker, saviour and demon – a bottle of Gordons Gin.

Staring, seeing, looking into light.

Sitting looking into the sun, one would automatically register that one was looking into a light. In depression, light, even if it exists, is a foreboding place, a place you want to avoid at all costs. It is a dark place. The light is not a light as it is merely a distraction from the darkness within oneself. It is not to be looked at with any meaning, for the light is for those that seek it.

In depression one does not seek anything other than the darkness. It is when one truly wants to see the light or even a glimmer of its existence, that one has made the first step towards recovery.

The refraction of the sun's rays and the rainbow it creates in a rain cloud symbolises the gradient of one's affliction of this devastating illness. The colours within it are moods and feelings that one cannot express and as each lighter colour emerges, so does one's ability to recognise the light that formed the rainbow in the first place. Newton expressed the rainbow as sevenfold, red, orange, yellow, green, blue, indigo and violet. At the end of a rainbow is a pot of gold. In a depressed mind, there is no pot of gold and there is no rainbow. It is just refraction of the sun against the water of life.

If you are happy and content in life there may be a pot of gold. For those of us who do not see life that way, it is a road, a pointer, a sign to nowhere and another of life's promises without substance. If one can move to reflecting on the brighter colours of the rainbow, one is nearer seeing the light that caused the beautiful apparition in the first place.

You cannot look directly at the sun and in a depressives' eyes, you cannot look at life as God gave it. Everything is so beautiful in God's creation, the colours, the flowers, the textures of nature's glory, hues and fragrances are all consuming; But only if you allow them to, or indeed want to see them that way! The world has a very dark side and as the sunlight fades, the darkness draws in. So does one's ability to take any comfort from the beauty that has drifted into shadow, even if one could see some comfort in the first place.

The sun's rays are too powerful to look at. Heat emitted from the core rebounds and takes centuries to come to the surface. Its power is 300,000 miles thick and a temperature of 6.5 million degree centigrade. In a depressed state, life itself is infinitely too bright to look at directly, and can appear just as thick to burrow into and as powerful to intrude upon. One lowers one's eyes from the brightness of the sun, knowing severe damage can result from the burning radiance that is emitted. When one is down, the experiences and 'happy' occasions that you should look forward to, and take pleasure from, become too bright, formidable and all consuming. One has to lower one's eyes.

What pleases, if you could call it that (maybe one could describe it as 'eases the pain'), is one's own ability to retreat into oneself. For you are safe there. Nothing can hurt you. You have the power of your own destiny, albeit, destiny is a million miles away from where you want to be. Now is now. Now is all consuming and nothing in the future can change that. Why would you want anything to change, for life is life and life is shit?

Even though one knows within oneself that there are beautiful, spectacular and breathtaking visions and experiences to take from the world, both in terms of nature and love, and power of emotion from relationships, they are all trivia, for nothing can take away that emotion of despair, loneliness and solitude. A depressive could be in a room with a loved one, a party with one hundred friends, at a concert with two thousand people who are merged and fused together for the love the same band. They could sit at The Theatre of Dreams with 76,000 Manchester United fans all united in their passion for their team.

It matters not. They are alone and that is all with which they are comfortable. Indeed the collective euphoria, happiness and togetherness can be debilitating and foreboding in its self. As the other 75,999 people are as one, have a common goal and are part of a tribal commune, you don't allow yourself the pleasure of that security, for you have no other commune than yourself.

The way I would describe severe depression to a lucky soul who has not had the experience of the dark side and Sir Winston Churchill's Black Dog, is similar to the death of a relative. One's utter despair at one's own inadequacies to have helped or assisted the deceased in the avoidance of the death, or righted wrongs, actually taken the time to speak to them for the first time in twenty years because of a dispute years previously, are all consuming.

You may only feel remorse that you maybe could have done more, maybe to have had a more fulfilling relationship, or if you had enjoyed a peace, solace and fulfilling relationship with that person, you have lost the friend, love, and soul to an outer spiritual life that you are not part of. You can no longer embrace the living entity, no longer comprehend their perception of life, no longer share in their experience, no longer touch them, feel them and be comforted by them. They have gone and memories, from the day they die are all you have to cling to.

Death of a loved one is heart breaking and destructive to the bereaved, as the loved one was part of their life in every way shape and form. The cadaver has no longer the soul to comfort, to entertain, to support or embrace, and loneliness for the one left behind, is now the only outcome. With that comes the feeling that this loneliness will last for an eternity, or at least until one dies oneself, thus relieving the excruciating pain that life without the loved one brings.

In depression, life itself has died.

CHAPTER TWELVE:

It's Time For The Nuthouse. (Are you surprised?)

You can't cross a chasm in two steps – Rashi Fein

The solution to my life occurred to me one evening while I was ironing a shirt – Alice Munro

The grand essentials to happiness in this life are something to do, something to love and something to hope for – Joseph Addison

<u>The following chapter was written following admission to the Priory. Whilst some of the commentary duplicates some of the previous chapter about depression, feelings and emotions etc, I felt it important that the reader experiences what it was like to be a part of that institution and have therefore not edited it in any way.</u>

<u>The following represents how I saw things in this very dramatic and hard time in my life.</u>

<u>By the way, most of it is funny so don't worry that you'll be re-visiting Accident and Emergency to have your wrist cuts sewn again. X</u>

Well, how life's rich tapestry can affect each and every one of us and to be perfectly honest one never can quite know when the bad side will come along and grab you by the balls and swing you around high in the sky stretching one's testis to the limit.

The mind can be a very dark and dangerous place and whilst it can all give us pleasure from the good things in life, it can also find weaknesses and infiltrate them with a steely cunning. In Dean Koontz's books, particularly those involving the mystical figure of Odd Thomas, he refers on many occasions to the Bodochs, intangible black shadows that breed on the weak and vulnerable and follow individuals that can be manipulated, invariably destined to die from the weakness, illness or destiny that invaded them in the first place.

Whilst the soliloquy possibly belies the boredom of the day (Sunday one does sod all, other than reflect on the previous week), it is a very difficult situation to explain to those who have not experienced the utter darkness of depression and any addictive illness.

Please bear with me with my expressive tendency, which, it has to be said, has been fully encouraged to assist in my recovery from both the aforementioned. To be perfectly honest, it does help and has assisted in the contribution to the unfinished book which has, no doubt, turned from a record of amusing anecdotes to a self help book for the clinically insane.

I was admitted to the Priory in February 2009. The Priory describes itself as an Acute Psychiatric Hospital and I was suffering from acute depression, alcohol addiction, panic attacks, anxiety and agitation not to mention a bit of obsessive compulsive disorder (OCD) to boot. If you are going to be ill, one might as well go for as many things as you can.

Anyway, Amy Winehouse recommended the Priory to me when I last saw her and thought that it must be good because she was looking as radiant and as beautiful as ever. I did ask Daddy if I had to go to rehab and he said, 'No, No, No!'. Well he didn't actually say that having died 31 years ago but I am sure he would have encouraged me. I therefore claim that he would have said, 'Yes, Yes, Yes!'

I must admit when I went in I was in a pretty bad condition and feel eternally grateful to my wife Rosa, who in many respects, should really have told me to 'fuck off' considering that I had left her a week beforehand. The demonic threatening beast known as depression has prowled upon my existence for many years and has been a grey and oppressive cloud heavier than gravity itself. Winston Churchill gave depression an identity and called it the Black Dog, something I referred to in the last chapter. The large black canine had decided to shit upon my head from a very great height and after a very large meal.

I was also having a fairly intoxicating romance, and affair. Unfortunately, this was not with a 19 year old blonde bombshell, originating from Helsinki, whose only addiction comprised lustful thoughts. I was having an affair with two very old men; Mr Gordon and Mr Schweppes to be exact, albeit I found them both very attractive and enjoyed far too many threesomes. I can assure you that I always practised safe sex with them, always using protection, via a slice of lemon and a couple of ice cubes.

The problem was that I was in a self imposed vulnerable position, somewhat daft for someone who needs people around me. Having left my wife of 25 years to seek peace and solitude, I was living at my sister Pip's house on my own at the time. She was in America developing her relationship with a white trailer man with a pick-up truck, a gun and a very large beard.

'You're going squeal like a pig,' and,

'You got a cute math, boy,' springs to mind albeit the film Deliverance was based and filmed in the deep South, not New England, although I suppose he could have driven the thousands of miles in between.

Anyway, I digress. The depression, anxiety, together with the increase in consumption to a bottle of Mr Gordon and 2 bottles of Mr Schweppes a day, started to take its toll in my lonely and uncertain state. This degenerated to such a degree, that intrusive thoughts started to infiltrate my sick mind, to find a place on the other side that had to be better than this. I will never forget that total lack of control that weekend I returned to my wife's house awaiting emergency, self admission to the nut house. I will always thank her for supporting me during this period when, in essence, we had separated.

On the Monday morning, we headed to the Priory and I was sure where it was. Unfortunately, the venue I was convinced would provide me with help and solace, was not the Acute Psychiatric Hospital, but Dunham Forest Golf Club. After 18 holes of glorious golf and 24 gin and tonics, completion of an application form and signing up to their 500 club, we set off again in search of the sobriotous haven of care, medication, group therapy and coffee.

Following a number of assessments by various people including the consultant, a doctor, a nurse and the head housekeeper who thought I was the new cleaner, I was placed in a group for addicts for whom the success of the hospital has an excellent reputation, albeit, one does like to go against the flow, just to be awkward but, hey ho, we will see. I was prescribed all sorts of pills and other potions many of which I looked forward to ordering on the internet upon my return home-wherever that was to be.

This was a fairly major disappointment to me to be on the addict course, as, whilst I would admit to being an alcoholic, I have always advocated that the depression caused the addiction but what do I know. Anyway the consultant stated that they always sort out the addiction before the depression as normally the depression is caused by the addiction. Just for the technical I will give you the Dictionary definitions as follows:

Alcoholism:

- A disorder characterised by the excessive consumption and psychological harm and impaired social and vocational functioning.

Addiction:

-Compulsive physiological and psychological need for a habit forming substance or action

or:

- The condition of being habitually or compulsively occupied with or involved in something.

That makes every boy and man over the age of twelve a total addict. An addict of the knob or dong or cock, however you wish to call it. Or in my case, chipolata!

Anyway, they advised me that many of my depressive, obsessive and agitated states would be addressed in the programme. However, should there be some issues remaining at the end, or identified during the course, they would be addressed. In other words they would undertake a 'mop up session'. My health care coverage was for twenty eight days and therefore it was important to get the diagnosis right. So, I was to be admitted to the 'Addiction Treatment Programme' the following day. I always then, and still do now, feel that I was placed on the wrong programme and once detoxed should have moved to the depression course. But hey, I'm a bank manager and not a psychiatrist!

The course was twenty eight days. Twenty eight days-bloody hell! I'm only a depressed alcoholic, not a bank securities clerk, who have to go on four week courses!!

I was led by the nurse to my room.

'I need to check your bag, Stephen.'

I suddenly realised I should have had a bath or shower prior to leaving home.

'You do realise that I have three?' I stated to the nurse worried that she would be concerned at the third testicle, which was diagnosed as a benign cyst a number of years ago by my Doctor. I pulled down my jeans and trousers, hoping that her hand would be warm, as any chill would have inverted my tiny manhood, concave, and turned my scrotum into rhino hide.

'No, your travel bag,' came the reply and I could just sense a slight smirk on the nurse's face as I popped away the chipolata in my embarrassment.

I emptied the contents of my bag, (that is travel bag and not the bag I was alluding to earlier), on to the bed and she started to rummage through the contents.

'What are you looking for?' I asked, wondering whether she was looking for donations to the local charity shop.

'Just things that you shouldn't bring in,' came the riposte.

I was so pleased that at the last minute I had decided to take out the Kalashnikov machine gun and that the blow up dolly with real hair and removable vagina was too exhausted from the night before to make the trip.

'Can't have this, or this, I'm afraid,' she insisted pulling out my belt from my packed trousers and my Mach 3 safety razor. I can see why I couldn't have the belt. She obviously was hoping that my trousers would fall down in front of some of her colleagues thus proving that I was as small as she was no doubt going to advertise on the staff notice board that afternoon.

However, I couldn't understand why I couldn't have my safety razor. Maybe, there was a direct correlation between the amount of facial hair one sported and the speed of recovery from the addiction or depression. However, this did not make complete sense as every drunk I have seen on the streets and depicted in films etc. had a huge, dirty beard which provided conservation breeding sites for various endangered species; it was therefore not for this reason.

'It is so that you can't harm yourself,' she explained, turning and walking out with the offending article and three bottles of gin that she had found hidden in my specially adapted platform shoes.

'See you later.'

I started to think about the razor. I know I had self-harmed prior to admission deciding that I would look far better with two black eyes. These had been completed in a very accomplished manner on the Saturday prior to admission in an anxiety attack and fit of agitation with the back of my hand.

I know now what self harm and an agitated state comprises. It isn't fun, it isn't in the USA and no one else is involved. It is one of the most frightening experiences I have encountered. You are just not in control of your body. There again, I have thought that every morning when naked, looking in the mirror dressing for work.

'Fuck sake boys!! Take cover; take cover, enemy fists attacking.' The armies they are attached and look somewhat toned and muscular.' - sorry pathetic joke but it fills another couple of lines.

I wonder how you can harm yourself with a safety razor.

'Dearly beloved, we are gathered here today to celebrate the life of Stephen Sheard who tragically died from shaving. His demise was lingering, taking him fourteen years and seven months to friction burn himself to death. My deepest sympathy goes out to his family and in particular his children, Gillette and Palmolive. One of the saddest things was that he never knew that his death was prolonged as a result of his ignorance of the ability to change the head.

'And at the setting of the sun and the five o'clock shadow, hair to hair, stubble to stubble I commend thy closely shaven body to God. May you rest in a hair piece.'

It's a bit daft really. You can have a wine glass in your room, (of course full of fresh orange), which if placed in a Tesco bag and hit with a very large book can provide hours of fun and pleasure playing noughts and crosses with oneself. Who needs paper when you have so much skin to abuse? (Sorry just a little tip I learnt from the self harm unit). By the way, if you get bored with noughts and crosses, you can always play the self-abuser's game of join the pimples, a variation of join the dots. By the time you are up to 77 pimples who gives a monkies what picture you can see developing.

On the first night I was settling in quietly lying on my bed at about 10.00 p.m. All was deathly quiet, no sound, other than various nocturnal wildlife, as it commenced its evening responsibilities. You know what it's like lying in bed on the first night of any hotel or hospital; comfortable but strange, safe, yet somewhat disconcerting, not knowing what lies in store.

Dingalingalingaling. An alarm - have I pressed a wrong button. No - it's a fire and it's not a drill - it's a bell.

'Don't panic, don't panic, Mr Mannering!'

The whole building was evacuated to the restaurant building while the fire brigade were called. I will never forget the sight as all occupants, whether depressed, spaced out, very thin, very fat, very old or very young, shuffled down the covered walkway. It was snowing hard that night and the procession contained every conceivable persona, slippers dragging, arms comforting themselves, to ward off the freezing cold.

The most tragic sight was the adolescents who are normally never seen. I will never forget one young girl, with beautiful strawberry blonde hair falling down her white dressing gown, a total lost soul, haunted eyes, staring into a void across the snow plain lawns. It was positively tragic and a memory that I will never forget until the day I die.

After half an hour, following the search by the boys in blue with yellow hats, the source of the alarms had been identified. An inmate had dried her curly black locks so fervently that she had almost set fire to her hair and the smoke from the kindling had wafted up to the fire alarms.

I, as most people, was somewhat shaken by the event, and following a number of fags returned to Odd Thomas and the comfort of my bed. Peace restored and gentle pace ensuing, I continued to flick through the pages embroiled in the story that unfolded, drifting, drifting drifting...

Peace broken, water flowing, a torrent somewhere, somewhere near, somewhere very near, hitting stone, concrete, tile brick..who knows?

I immediately rose from the bed and ran into the bathroom expecting the ceiling to be embracing the floor in a messy clinch. However, all that was raging causing the torrent, was the powerful shower attached to the wall. The shower had turned itself on of its own volition, possibly the plastic bath demanding refreshment and cleansing. The shower controller was a sensor based affair. All one had to do was place a hand over the sensor and it would power up either for the bath or shower depending upon the sensor sensitised and at a designated temperature. But what had set it off? A fly, a spider? There was nothing there, no insect of any description whatsoever adorned any wall or surface in the bath or adjacent walls. I turned the shower off and returned to the bed even more disquieted than upon arrival in the hospital itself.

Depressives, especially those with obsessive tendencies, can experience intrusive thoughts which can run wild. Reading Koontz's book with the Bodochs, my mind started to wander.

Had some previous patient and occupant in the room taken one's life in the bathroom and its soul had failed to pass to the other side? A poltergeist's angst was focused on the bathroom's new occupant, unhappy that he would not maintain his physical appearance having no ability to shave, the power of the beast unleashed.

The previous occupant had used a dressing gown belt. She used a slipknot, tied it around the shower head embedded in the wall, attaching the opposite end around her neck. Allowing the ligature to slowly tighten, she slid down the wall, triggering the shower sensor.

Water cascaded from the shower head, rivulets steaming down the tie, into the hair and down her face, racing down her naked body into the bath below. As her legs lowered, the water changed direction across her body, following different paths, creating new tributaries, joining old ones, creating new ones, legs sinking down and down, until the ligature stretched to its maximum tension.

Further and further the legs descended, the face bloating, eyes starting to pop, the ligature doing the job for which it was intended. Death's dark veil finally came to bear.

I found out the following day that it was nothing to do with Mrs Poltergeist. Apparently, when no one uses the shower for a number of days, it has a computer chip which triggers a self-cleaning programme and will come on to keep the pipes functioning.

Just shows that I didn't have a shower on my first day. 'I know, I know but when you are depressed you are allowed not to look after yourself!'

Another thing I couldn't get my head around during the first few days was that you had to be accompanied every time you went to the restaurant which is situated in a different building. They say that this is in case you have fits in detox.

'Bollocks,' (all three of them).

They just want to know whether you had the pork or the chicken.

Another thing which was equally irritating was that the nurses come and check you are still in the building, or in the lounge, or in your bed, every thirty minutes for the first five days of your stay - even during the night.

It makes it therefore impossible to ever do anything one shouldn't do which lasts more than twenty nine minutes. A side effect of anti-depressant drugs is that it suppresses the ejaculation trigger when making love or enjoying a little DIY. It was therefore impossible to achieve any sexual gratification whatsoever within this very short timescale. The chicken was therefore not choked, and the Bishop avoided a bashing, (however you wish to describe it). How would you go on if you were in the sex addiction detox unit?

On the second or third night, I was getting rather miffed at my incarceration and considered hiding, maybe under the bed or above the roof tiles, when I knew the snooping Thomases were due. This would cause maximum panic and disruption, but I never had the bottle to do it.

I also had the thought that I might lie in a strange position on the floor as the night nurse came in, eyes wide open and unblinking. This would have been a step too far, however, if the cow that laughed at my manhood is ever on night watch, who knows!!

I had to have vitamin substitutes whilst in The Priory, which incidentally were administered through an extraordinarily large needle in the rectum rather than voluntary oral intake. It was labelled the Rhino needle by the addicts and administered at approximately 9.00 p.m. You could always tell who had just experienced this as one's gait told the story. Following the injection it appeared that one side of the bottom was in complete seizure.

It absolutely killed and they alternated the injection every night, left then right, when one had to bare ones bottom to the nurse. Regrettably, the administerer tended to be male or ugly females and the females were far better at administration than the males.

I think the males were practising for the local darts team as they tended to stand around 7' 3" away and aim at treble twenty which invariably hit double three. The worst was when they split the wire on 11 – a joke that will only mean anything to a dart player but I am sure you can imagine the repercussions.

We had some fantastic laughs and some deep emotional trauma in that place and to be quite honest the range of strugglers became my family. It is amazing how far the emotion spectrum and its nadir and zenith can be so far apart. It is also so surprising how you feel the nadir has come, only to find that 'Nadir Football Club's' goal posts have been moved.

Just before, during and after my stay in the Priory, I reached lows that could only be described as unbearable. Not one iota of self worth, purpose, confidence or motivation.

We were divided into two groups on my floor, which was the lower floor of the building, and two groups on the top floor. On the ground floor were those suffering from chronic depression / depression and any addictions, whilst on the top floor which is totally separate, the eating disorders unit and the child unit. There were a total of fifty three beds of which six were for the adolescents.

Apparently there were circa one hundred and twenty staff for the patients and therefore the staff / patient ratio was quite staggering. I suppose at £625 per night with a course lasting twenty eight days they could afford it. In addition the place was half empty, the atmosphere gentle, caring, loving and ideal for recovery. (On the proviso that one wanted to become better, which may sound ridiculous, however, we are talking about seriously ill psychological patients here, not those recovering from a lanced boil).

I did attempt to commit suicide upon my admission by jumping out of the window only to find that I was actually standing very slightly higher than the floor in the room I had jumped out of. I did complain about this appalling lack of fore-thought when designing the acute psychiatric ward and they asked me if I wanted a transfer to another clinic.

'Well,' I said. 'I have heard from a deceased friend about short breaks in Switzerland at a hotel called Dignitas. I have heard though that the food comes in short supply and room service is all that it is not cracked up to be. They haven't even got knives and forks and prefer to use plastic tubes for feeding.'

I also noted that everything in the room in the Priory was specifically designed not to allow one to kill oneself. For example the two bedside lamps were screwed to the worktop and the lead was only just long enough to reach the plug socket. The best was the telephone. This was doctored to such a degree that you almost had to rest your head on the table upon which it sat to talk or listen into the receiver. There was nothing to hang oneself on or with, and I thought that this was a very poor show considering the amount of money one was paying.

So, as I said, depressives and the addicts were on the bottom floor. I felt that I was developing a dual personality as I did not know which way to go in the morning. Do I follow the depressives or the addicts? I tell you what, it does your head in so much, and it's enough to put you in an institution! There is some evidence that I suffer from a split personality and this was helpful as I could attend two classes in the two separate areas of the building at the same time. The only down side was that I couldn't decide whether I was depressed about being dry or happy that I was depressed.

One evening at around 9.30 p.m., I decided to cut my hair with my old clippers. I could just about see into the mirror in the bathroom with the plug, plugged into the socket in the bedroom. I have been having a small problem over the last year or so with the clippers, however, everything seemed to be working fine with balls of grey / mousey hair falling into the toilet basin. I did the right hand side of my hair and rose from the bounds of the toilet basin and looked for missed bits.

Everything was going so well and I turned on the clippers to do the left side. I swept the vibrating clipper through my aging locks and shook it out into the toilet. However, no hair departed. I did this again and once again there was no hair to be seen. It was still making the correct noise and the head was still vibrating but still no locks came a tumbling.

I turned it off and adjusted the No 2 selected clipper attachment to see whether this had become dislodged in the process, however this was not the case and I reattached it. Once again nothing happened.

My hair had grown to about an inch and I was presented with a closely shaved right side and a relatively full head of hair on the left. After approximately one hour of frustration, I bashed the offending vibrating clipper so hard on the floor that it disintegrated and is now in a local landfill site.

So by this time it was approximately 11.15 p.m. and there was no one about other than the night porter and a few night nurses, (the living kind rather than the ones you take for a cold).

'Hi Graham, I don't suppose you have or know where you can get me any clippers do you?' I stated in a frantic tone, attempting to cover my head with my hand and duck low enough below the nurse's station counter not to be seen.

'No idea Stevie boy,' came the retort from the Scottish concierge and I ran back to my room. I ended up spending the next two hours shaving off the left hand side of my 1 inch hair with the safety razor I had been allowed back, only to realise that now I had a totally bald patch on the left hand side of my head and 2mm of hair on the other.

Finally I put shaving cream all over my head and shaved the lot off.

Now whilst this is a rather silly story and one which probably does not warrant the time it took to write it, I do feel that I have let an ideal opportunity go by, from which I could have had a little fun.

A number of in patients suffered from dual personalities and I think I could have made a very special test case in the therapy group in question. By turning one's head as quickly as possible from one side to the other I could have caused total confusion and I have seen this done with beards in the past and also clothes where one side is a woman's set of clothes and the other a man's, with the associated hair styles. What confusion could reign in the dual personality unit with this type of head attire and I am sure that the Priory will be looking into this type of therapy in the future to bolster their coffers from extended stays.

However, all this does not beat the story of the drunk who decided to drink a bottle of scotch on the way in the Priory. This was a classic. Not only totally inebriated, he was given various mind numbing drugs upon admission, and was called to be escorted for his evening meal. 'I'll be through in a few minutes,' he slathered, 'I just need a shave.'

With hands trembling with the shakes he took out his Palmolive shaving cream and safety razor which he had been allowed in the room for 10 minutes for the purpose of shaving off the ¼ inch stubble that adorned his face. Rather than applying the shaving cream to his face, he is alleged to have placed the cream on the mirror, exactly where his face reflected. He then proceeded to shave the face on the mirror. It is likely that this gentleman is now in the Labour Cabinet where one would expect this kind of behaviour.

There were some very interesting sub-divisions within each of the sections. For example, the depressives included those that could not get over the fact that there were not sufficient packets of biscuits available, in between the seventeen meals that were provided every day. Many had the equivalent of a Somerset dairy farm herd's lard extraction, embodied into their bottoms and complained that they were struggling with their thyroid. Just stop eating and get thinner you fat bitch!!

Others, upstairs, who suffered from eating disorders of the thin kind, had bigger rooms than us according to the nurses. Why did they have bigger bedrooms? They were in the eating disorders unit and they were all half the size they should be. I think it was because they occasionally were visited by the depressives and had to accommodate bottoms the size of a small English county on the bedroom chair.

They also had the benefit of twenty seven meals a day albeit each comprised one Heinz baked bean. They also didn't eat with the depressives or the addicts. Unfortunately, the queues for the food were getting far too long in the main restaurant and the food was going cold before any of it was touched.

I named the depressives, 'The Glums' and the addicts the 'Wine Glums'. The Wine Glums were the ones with any form of humorous riposte whatsoever. That is why the Glums and the Wine Glums were encouraged to share the same living room. You could always tell the two apart even though they were interspersed.

The Glums were the ones with the unhappy faces, drugged to the eyeballs, normally with very large bottoms, surrounded by Penguin biscuit wrappers. They also never stopped comparing how many milligrams of medication they were on – the more they were on, the more respect they received. They also knew every possible medication known to man, the effect that it had on each and every one of them, along with any side effects.

They were also so fucking miserable!!!

The Wine Glums always had a coffee or a bottle of coke in their hands. Whilst they had an excellent sense of humour they were very jealous of the Glums, mainly due to the copious amount of medication that they received on a regular basis. As most addicts have totally addictive personalities, if one has not been able to drink, take cocaine etc. for any considerable time, it is amazing how attractive the medical station medicine cupboard becomes.

There was one dizzy dispenser of a woman who was always flustered if more than one in-mate went to the counter at any one time. Each person's medicine was placed in a tiny little pot with another equally sized little pot of water, to down the various pills which came in various shapes and sizes. The nurse had to watch the patient take the prescribed medicine in front of her in order that she could confirm that the recipient had, for one, taken the prescribed pills and two, they were not hiding the aforementioned under their tongue, to store up thus allowing either a massive high, low or suicide attempt; or indeed sell on the Wine Glum black market.

The Wine Glums thought it would be a wheeze to make sure we all arrived whilst the Glums were also at the counter, try to distract the recipient and rush dizzy Lizzie into speedy provision.

The idea would then be to quickly turn over all the pots (excluding water) and mix them up really quickly – a little like the performing magician who can always lose one ball from three or transfer it to another container. This would result in a huge pick and mix, take it as it comes free for all, where chaos would ensue. Maybe that is why Woolworths went bust. Their pick and mix comprised only sweets.

The Glums could be high as kites whilst the addicts could audition for Michael Jackson's Thriller video. Carnage! Fantastic!

There was also a pecking order within the Wine Glum community. There were two criteria, dependant on the number of AA meetings they had attended and the number of rhino injections you had endured. I was mid table on the latter having endured five arse benders, the dosage of which ranged from three to seven injections. The AA meetings I have to say I hadn't done too well with. I found them intolerable and possibly the most boring meetings I have ever attended in my 48 years on this dismal planet.

AA and the twelve step programme is very much central to the addiction program I was attending. Therefore, the Priory not only laid on AA meeting and aftercare meetings for us and previous sufferers to attend, but also we visited AA meetings outside the grounds.

We were transported in one of those vans that transports prisoners from the court house to the jail. The windows were blacked out in order that we could not see any public houses on the way and we had an armed guard to ensure safe passage. (Not really! We went in a minibus and the driver was not open to bribes – we tried!!)

The ideology of AA is to help anyone with an alcohol problem and it obviously works looking at the numbers of people in attendance. It relies on one wishing to stop, acknowledging the damage that alcohol is doing to oneself and others, and then gives great support through the meetings which are all over the world.

'My name's Crispin and I'm an alcoholic!'
'Hello, Crispin,' the gathering replied.
'I went on holiday to the The Congo Basin last week and was able to attend an AA meeting within the local terrorist encampment. I found it very humbling and encouraging that Second Chief Bottawotang had given up drinking the blood of the local goat, over four years ago.'

'Thank you Crispin for your story and thank you for sharing this with the fellowship.'

The meetings were variable in both content and worth, but I have to say when they were bad they were very bad.

I went to one, one and a half hour aftercare meeting. Its sole purpose was to ensure that the braincells became so bored and crinkled that the Priory could offer other courses and therapies at £625 per night. I think the sixty or so attendees were from the local Brain Dead Unit. Talking is good. Talking for talking sake of talking is like wiping ones bottom after a dump until the only deposit is the blood from the piles the tissue was there to cleanse.

Of the sixty people there, only four people talked and the same four said exactly the same thing that they had said at the other AA meeting and aftercare groups I had been to. The other fifty six people were all in differing states of inertia.

The range of snores, grim looks, staring into space was positively the most interesting part. One man actually stated that there were exactly one hundred and twenty six ceiling tiles covering the room of infuriating boredom. My initial reaction was to actually see whether he was right and realised quickly that this was going to be true, as he stated how many tiles comprised each section of the roof prior to each lintel that supported the roof voids.

Anyway, it did keep my mind occupied for a significant period lasting approximately 29 seconds, which in the grand scheme of things, was a welcome respite.

This meeting was supposed to bring together those who were in an early stage of recovery of, in this case, alcohol addiction, and to be perfectly honest, I felt that the main sponsor for the event was Bells whiskey. I had been dry for 11 days by then, an achievement which has never been experienced in the Sheardie liver for many years. I had no cravings, not even a hint of a wish to engage in the devil's liquid during my stay other than twice. Both of these occasions occurred at the end of the meetings and to be quite frank, if there had been a bottle of Gordons available, the contents would have been downed within seconds.

I will give you an idea of the content of the meeting mentioned above as follows:

The hour and a half meeting began with the usual introduction asking for people to share and ask questions for debate.

The bible of those seeking sobriety via AA is the twelve steps and its rules, missions, statements and goals are all laid out in what is known as, 'The Big Book.'

The first debate comprised was about how many times the document, which was written in the early twentieth century by a drunken doctor and a drunken stockbroker,

(a period when religion was somewhat deemed more important than it is now), stated the word God in its 100 or so pages.

'No it actually says it six times,' came the reply.

'Yes but in 1955, it was re-written with the caveat on the back stating that 'God' was to be seemed and deemed as whatever 'tickles your fancy',' (not in those words exactly but you know what I mean).

'But should an attendee at an AA meeting be allowed to prophesied about God's help in abstinence?'

This debate went on and on and on and on and on to the point where people were starting to remove their 'I've been in the AA for 120 years and attended 2,000,678,567 meetings' badge adorning their jacket lapel, and slowly insert the one inch pin into the centre of their eyeball. After this dastardly deed was completed, they obviously decided that the pain was less than that experienced in the meeting and proceeded to pull the offending sharp out of their eyeball and insert it into the other, knowing that at least this would take up another 8 minutes of purgatory. Eight minutes less of hell to endure.

My only synopsis is that it is the meeting itself, and not the content, is there to assist those who suffer from alcohol abuse. As meeting are scattered around various areas, this means that sufferers (of the meetings) not from the illness, have to travel copious amounts of miles to attend, maybe twenty to forty miles in some cases. This no doubt will take anything up to an hour to complete.

The meeting then is a purgatorial ninety minutes, then, a quick coffee to waken up from the deep sleep, and another one hour back home. This means that sixty attendees are not able to drink for four hours. What a fantastic way to keep people from the dreaded sup of their choice.

Many people are proud that they attended 90 meetings following detox, in 90 days and many try to go to meetings five times a week. In addition, many people have been going to these meetings for a period of up to thirty years.

WHY? I would rather be found dead in a pool of my own vomit, twenty seven times over the drink driving limit, than be destined to a life of AAdom. At least I would have had a bloody decent night.

We were not just a bunch of alcoholics in our therapy group; we also had other ranges of friends. We all had addictive personalities and it is how, and in what format, these come out depending upon your trait, opportunity, leaning or devil. The desperation of the illness is such that the addiction can change over the years from one aspect of life or substance to another, or be prevalent across many. I have the greatest respect for the professionals in this area of medicine. To unravel one's brain must be so incredibly difficult and has to be a bit hit and miss on occasions as people are very good at covering up or find it difficult to eloquently express how they feel for the doctors to make a diagnosis.

If you break a leg, it is quite obvious how to diagnose, treat and make good, however, one's mind has so many facets and differing traits, that it must be so hard to not only diagnose but also how best to change that particular way of thinking.

We had cocaine addicts - 'How do they smell?' I hear you cry.

'Bloody awful!' came the reply. Still, if they were into piercings, it saves on the one in the nose.

Workaholics! I think that these must be the most poorly and clinically insane of all of us. Who would want to get up at three, then four, then five, then six in the morning, to see what e-mails they have received, knowing that they cannot respond back, or certainly the response won't be read until 9.30 the next morning.

The most interesting one is the sex addict.
'Fucking marvellous,' I hear you all say, and boys, on occasions, these can be women.

'Bloody Hell! Book me in for another 28 days.'

Well sod's law had it that I could not find any such addict during my stay either male or female which was more than a little disappointing. However, what did provide great amusement was how one was treated and we did spend hours debating this. The detox, normally in the case of an addict would consist of reducing number and amounts of appropriate drugs. But what about the sex addict.

After a full discussion we decided that it should take the following format as follows, and please bear in mind that this is geared to a man, but could equally be adapted to a woman. My eight day detox program would be as follows:

Day 1: Full unadulterated hardcore pornography dispensed at nine o'clock a.m., twelve o'clock p.m., six o'clock p.m. and ten o'clock p.m.

One Viagra tablet to be administered orally, at a time to be discussed with the consultant. Tissues would be dispensed upon request to save on housekeeping bills and the dry cleaning of curtains.

Day 2: Soft pornography dispensed at the same times with half a Viagra tablet with rough cheap toilet paper upon request.

Day 3: Issue of the Daily Sport at nine o'clock a.m., the Sun at twelve o'clock p.m., the Star at six o'clock p.m. and a choice of Fiesta magazine or Readers' wives over 30 at ten o'clock p.m., with the previous newspaper to mop up the slops. A quarter of one Viagra tablet at a time to be discussed with the consultant.

Day 4: No further Viagra, a copy of the Sunday people issued at lunch time and a copy of Readers' Wives over 60 at night time.

Day 5: A box set of the New Avengers which can be viewed at will but lights out and cock down at 10.00 p.m.

Day 6: She magazine to be issued and should additional material be requested for relapse purposes, Woman's Own

Day 7: A box set of Last of the Summer Wine with additional counselling surrounding Nora Batty's stockings, encouraging the patient to be strong during their revealing.

Patient to be encouraged to think of alternative events during these difficult times, to include questions like who won the world cup in 1954.

Day 8: Patient to be fully clothed in ski wear with hands tied to the bed head for the full 24 hours.

What amazed me in my stay in the Acute Mental Hospital to give it its proper name were the differing types of people. Mind games do not distinguish between the old and young, colour or creed, gender or sexual orientation. Is it sadder that a sixty two year old man comes in for treatment for alcohol addiction and is diagnosed with sclerosis of the liver and one more drink will kill him? Or the twenty five year old girl who binge drinks for four days in a row, kept awake with cocaine? Both are tragic cases, however neither may die from their addiction or both may. It is the one that is strong enough to accept that they have possibly the most untreatable illness of the lot and does something about it.

That something is, without doubt, total abstinence and a will not to indulge in any activity that will encourage a cross addiction. Both are huge hurdles to cross.
The twenty eight day programme was strange in that one could join at any time and generally involved around eight to ten inmates. There were therefore, at any one time, people at the early stage and those who were just about ready to leave.

The dynamics of the group constantly changed from those who were still in detox and fairly spaced out to those who were supposedly 'cured' and were about to break out of the Priory bubble back into real life and a life of AAdom, NAdom, CAdom etc.

The typical day comprised a set format for the majority of the time. 9.30 a.m. to 10.30 a.m. was interpretation and emotions arising from a daily meditation book, which sounds rather boring but the readings did evoke many different feelings for different people. Some of the quotations which triggered discussion are in this book under each chapter heading, written in italics.

Then each person had to read out their daily diary from the day before and feedback was provided. This covered whether it was a good day, indifferent day or bad day and the reasons why. The diary also included what you had learned and what you wished to improve. After the break and up to lunch was normally a video or presentation on an aspect of addiction.

Lunch was 12.30 p.m. until 2.00 p.m. In the afternoons, depending upon where you were up to in the programme, a certain revelation or 'step' was completed by an individual. The first one was to read out your life story. Many of these were totally heartbreaking and it was a daily occurrence that the Scottie box of tissues would be passed around the room.

Step One was equally hard where the individual had to read out in a specific format how their addiction of choice had affected every aspect of their life, for example, home, family, work, legal aspects, friends, mental state etc. At the end of this, they were given unopened letters from any family members or friends who had taken the trouble, when asked a few days earlier, to complete and forward in for the session.

As you would expect, to read a letter from a loved one as to how the addiction had affected them having not read it previously, created emotional turmoil, not just for the person reading it, but more often than not, all in the room. It was at this point on day eighteen that I did this step and also proved to be the day I decided that the course was not going to help me further.

This particular step was to acknowledge that you had a problem with addiction, which I of course recognised. However, part of the step was to acknowledge that you were powerless to help yourself and wanted to rid yourself completely of the drug, the actions, or juice of your choice. Well this is the part that I really struggled to come to terms with. I just wasn't ready to state that alcohol was affecting my life as badly as it could and I certainly wasn't in a position to say that I would commit or even try to give it up completely at the end of the course.

Step Two and Step Three were steps where you acknowledged that you could not do this on your own and committed to a 'higher power' to assist you stay sober or clean. The words 'Higher Power' obviously came up for scrutiny, however, merely refers to either the power of the group, AA group or God if you have one.

I have to say that the course was emotionally gruelling, where everyone would spill out feelings and events that they had never shared with anyone before. Many of these were truly heartbreaking and at the end of the day you were knackered.

I pity every person on this planet that has an addictive personality, as to surmount the illness there is the highest mountain to climb to keep away from temptation at every level. An analogy has been made that the addict is on a lift with sobriety on the top floor, however, there are hundreds of floors on the way up, each with its own temptation. We all attempt to travel to the top, however only 3% ever reach it on their first attempt. A very sobering thought.

Many funny stories came out during my twenty one days in the Priory. I know, I know, it was a twenty eight day programme, but more of that later. Some of these came from the Glums and some came from the Wine Glums. By the way, we did re-name both at one stage to the 'Pissed Offs' and the 'Pissed Ups'.

Some of the more unusual tales related to how alcoholics can keep their habit secret. It is a well known fact that the addict becomes devious and lies often to convince others, mainly loved ones or work colleagues, that they do not drink anything like the amount they do. One woman who drank five bottles of wine a day but lived alone used to get up at 6.00 a.m. on bottle collection day to distribute the thirty five bottles from the previous week around neighbour's bottle containers. This gave her some comfort that even the bin men did not know how far she had fallen.

Another man kept a bottle of gin at work in the first aid cupboard.

One story which was told to us by an ex-addict in one session involved a man who drank copious amounts of vodka and his wife was threatening divorce unless he stopped. He tried and failed but realised that he would no longer be able to have bottles around the house. The ingenuity of his deceit beggars belief.

Up in the loft he installed a twenty litre water bottle complete with dispenser, like the ones that adorn the floors of most offices and waiting rooms. In the empty bottle he placed twenty litres of finest Russian vodka tipping it up and placed it into the hopper. From the plastic tap he attached a long plastic tube. He then proceeded to drill a hole through the loft floor into his bedroom. The hole was concealed behind fitted wardrobes.

The tube was then pushed through the loft floor and down into the wardrobe. He used cable clips to neatly fasten the tube to the wall ensuring that it could not be seen. The tube was then passed through the arm of an old coat which hung in the corner and a further plastic tap attached at the end of the cuff. Finally the tap in the loft was turned on and he could access the vodka by turning the tap in his coat.

His wife must have thought he must have had a lover the amount of time he spent deciding which clothes to wear. It was brilliant and desperately sad at the same time.

A similar story of deceitfulness, but brilliantly conceived, concerned the man who loved to do up old cars. His wife was obviously totally happy that he had a pastime which took his mind off his drinking and encouraged him to restore the vehicle to his heart's content.

What she wasn't aware of was how he always appeared a little glassy eyed upon his return from the garage then when he had gone out. She had searched the workshop and the garden, high and low for hidden bottle, to no avail. She obviously also did not appreciate the ingenuity of her husband.

Once a week, when his wife was out completing the weekly shop, he would purchase 5 litres of Teachers whisky and empty the contents into the windscreen washer container of the car he was restoring. He would immediately dispose of the bottles down at the local bottle bank.

He had blocked off one of the squirters which covered the left hand side of the windscreen so that it could not eject any fluid. However, the one on the right hand side was turned sideways at an angle such that he could reach the windscreen washer push button on the windscreen wiper stick. By pressing the button with his left hand and holding his head at a certain angle, the Scottish nectar was forced into his mouth.

The final story which caught my attention was the man who used to take his dog for a walk at least three times a day. His wife had no interest in the dog and therefore never walked it, however, she started noticing that whenever her husband returned from the walk, he smelt of drink and was somewhat unstable on his feet. She began to suspect the inevitable.

However, there were no shops or off licences within walking distance of their house, only open fields and parkland, and the woman could not understand how he could become so intoxicated.

Where on earth was he getting the drink?

This went on for many months and her husband continued to appear to be deteriorating. When asked, he would just totally deny any wrongdoing. Then one day he became ill; just a bad case of the flu, however, he was certainly not in a position to walk his beloved dog.

Grudgingly, his wife decided that it was unfair for the dog not to be walked and attached its lead. She knew roughly where her husband walked the dog as she had watched him out of the upstairs window to see whether he reached for a bottle in a pocket. He never did though!

At the usual spot the dog was let off the lead. The canine started to spring through the grasslands and open spaces with gay abandon loving the freedom that his master's partner had allowed. However, he would not respond to her calling and seemed to be pulling her in a certain direction.

She walked up an incline and at the top of the ascent saw a small copse of trees below. She scanned the forestation and saw the dog sitting bolt upright, wagging his tail frantically staring up at an old oak. Wondering if he had spotted a squirrel or some other creature to chase and hunt down, she wandered up to the dog and looked up into the tree. Approximately four feet up the trunk of the withered giant was a large hole. Looking into it, what did she find?

A box of dog biscuits.

Delving a little further in and fearing that a squirrel might suddenly like the look of her pinky, she carefully felt around. Five minutes later she had lined up a box of Chappie tit bits, three empty one litre bottles of Gordons finest, and six and a half full bottles of Gordons finest.

'But was the half full one, half full or half empty?' I hear you ask.

I suppose that would depend on whether you were a depressive or not, however, one minute later it was fully empty as were the other six. I never did get to know what happened to the dog biscuits and presume they formed the staple diet of her husband's tea that evening.

All these stories just emphasise the lengths addicts will go to, to suppress their craving and hide their best friend from family.

How about a Glum story?

One Glum had great difficulty in having a plop. For a week she had been struggling and it was starting to cause her even more upset. How true this was, and any Doctor which may be reading this story may say that is crap, (no pun intended), but she decided that the leading end of the turtles head was so hard that she couldn't pass a motion. Bit like the Labour Party in more ways than one!

She therefore decided to use a teaspoon to try to dislodge the offending log end. How successful she was in doing this is unclear. Whilst I gather she did dispose of the teaspoon in an appropriate manner, one of the other Glums misinterpreted its disposal and advised one of the nursing staff that she had placed the spoon into the dishwasher. All hell broke loose as three nurses dived into the communal kitchen to empty the contents into the bin.

If the offending article had been placed in the dishwasher and not been washed, it would have brought a completely new meaning whilst sampling the delights of the coffee machine.

'One lump or two, Marjorie?'

The Glums had bespoke programmes depending upon their prognosis. Some were only in for a couple of weeks whilst others had been there for twelve weeks or more. One girl, who will obviously remain nameless was from Liverpool and swore like a trooper. If ever you were running dialect and diction courses, she would have been an astounding example of a Scouser: brash, loud, funny and the strongest accent ever.

Even though it was 'The Priory', the choice of the stars, the language occasionally beggared belief. Virtually anybody could say anything to anybody and it was seen as part of the healing process, aiding interaction and promoting inter-personal skills.

If it was outrageous, one could always blame it on the fact that you were in an acute psychiatric unit and were suffering from the illness your mind had allowed to enter. However, this led to some unbelievable discussions almost too 'top shelf' to print.

The girl from Liverpool was sitting at the dinner table one day and it was packed. Bear in mind that this was run akin to a proper restaurant, and guests and consultants joined the merry, or un-merry throng to dine.

She started with her tale emanating from the yoga and relaxation class that she had attended with some six other Glums.

'Dat fukkun woman who runs that relaxation class, she does me fukkun ead in.'

The whole restaurant audience stopped chewing, cutting, drinking, choosing, talking, sipping, to hear what was coming next from the booming tirade from the girl suffering from irritable dialect syndrome.

'We were all on mats, rite, fukkin lying on our backkkks and she told us all to raise our legs in the air. When I did it, I let out the biggest fukkin fanny fart yuv ever eard.

She gave me the dirtiest fuccun look you've ever seeeen.'

The whole dining room was quieter than the reference library on Manchester's Oxford Road. You could hear a pea fall off a fork. But, alas, there was more!

'Anyway, the fukkun teecha then lay down and she fukkun let out an even bigger one, I thought her fanny was going to explode. I fukkun nearly pissed laughing.'

The Glums, the Wine Glums and the waitresses all cried with laughter. Many of the guests looked shocked and the three consultants who were sitting eating with the yoga and relaxation teacher were mortified.

I have no idea what happened to the Yoga teacher, albeit I have no doubt that she is in one of the other Priorys as an in-patient, hopefully with her front bottom still intact.

There was an older chap in the Wine Glums who was by all accounts a fairly poorly man and not one which should be encouraged to attend a wine tasting session for his own good. He was a master of understatement, never really contributing to the many group sessions that comprised the course, other than cringe-worthy comments made on a fairly regular basis.

For example, on one occasion, one of the in-mates had described that not only did she suffer from alcoholism but also had an eating disorder. It later transpired that the girl suffered from bulimia, a condition where food is consumed and then one throws it back up into the ceramic toilet bowl.

The girl was sobbing as she told her story and at the end of it there was silence.

'Do ya just not like food then?' broke the air with a knife so sharp it could cut a rock in half, from our fellow in crime.

On another occasion he would not believe that a lesbian in our group, sporting very short spiky hair and as butch as they come, was in actual fact a woman.

'That's never a woman, it's a bloke!' was his contribution on her first day in therapy. It transpired that the girl from a very early age felt that she was a man in a woman's body – truly saddening. This chap was a loose cannon indeed!

One of his most famous faux pax emanated from his first evening whilst still intoxicated by the two bottles of whisky he had drunk in the previous twenty four hours. He apparently was lying in bed still fairly drunk as a skunk and noticed the square electrical box next to the bedside cabinet with a red button in the centre. Reaching out with a shaking hand he pressed the button and waited.

Alarm bells sounded at the nurse's station and within seconds there were white coats and blue trousers running down the tranquil corridors breaking what inner peace and solace all the residents had gleaned from that day. Sprinting nurses and assistants came from every direction, congregating outside the man's room. The senior nurse took charge, quickly knocked and entered, expecting to find the occupant in the midst of a heart attack, or a stroke, or that he had fallen badly. Something had gone wrong, and it was something bad.

'Can I have a cup of coffee, white with two sugars, love?' he requested.

Now, this would be a nice little story in itself, however it does generate an element of concern, indeed trepidation, when you are aware of his employment.

Obviously highly intelligent once in his life, before the ravages of brain cell destruction through alcohol-induced coma had commenced, the gentleman in question had built up a fairly large engineering business, specialising in pressure vessels. When we say vessels, we maybe conjure up an image of a measuring jug. No, in this case, a vessel was a huge container which a man had to enter to clean.

He openly declared that he had designed, built and installed vessels of varying sizes and purposes for Sellafield nuclear processing plant. This is no doubt that the author's imagination is running wild, but could you imagine if he was in charge of the final testing process.

I know nothing of the industry, other than significant detail, both technical, and aspects of infrastructure, gleaned from Homer Simpson in 'The Simpsons' working at the Springfield nuclear power station. There is always a red button in the middle of the wall or table that shut downs or melt downs the whole plant. Let's hope he didn't want a coffee when working there! Having said that I think he was on holiday during the final throws of completion and testing at Sellafield.

It probably was what is known as a 'busman's holiday'. After leafing through the pages of various travel brochures he found an ideal one:

'Saga Nuclear Installations in Europe and Eastern Europe'.

'Why not stay in the darkness of an eight foot square concrete bunker and take daily trips around our site. Full protective clothes will be provided and as much oxygen from our specially designed Saga lightweight cylinders as you require.

'You'll love meeting new friends with a common interest in nuclear physics and particle bombardment. Here at Chernobyl, you can upgrade your bunker to a Stateroom with eight inch reinforced porthole window, overlooking the main reactor for an extra £275. This ten day all-inclusive trip, includes free Geiger counter readings every hour and, as a special once in a lifetime offer, ten free pairs of Russian underpants with our logo emblazoned on the side.'

I was surprised at this free gift as I was always told that you should never wear Russian underpants because Chernobyl fall out!!!

A couple of the in-mates on the addiction programme were gay. Not wishing to sound homophobic in any way, but I had never really had much experience of those who lean in a direction opposite to the mainstream. Not wishing to be disrespectful or patronising in any way, but I do feel that the additional pressure of finding you are in a minority must lead to significant additional pressure in life, particularly during the teen years when one is so vulnerable.

'Coming out', must be so difficult, and on many occasions must not only have a ripple effect across families and friends who never had any idea, but also be dreadfully difficult psychologically for the person themselves.

I also found these inmates, both male and female, the friendliest and funniest of the lot. What I could not get my head around was the way, in particular, the decadent way in which they talked and acted, both male and female. I have to say that I found them bawdier than probably every testosterone induced rugby player on a tour of Soho I've ever met.

One was telling me of her admission. At admission, all electrical appliances, for example phone chargers, have to be PAT tested. No idea on earth what that means but presume they are tested to ensure they are safe to use and by plugging in the appliance there is no danger of fire or explosion.

The man who did this testing was an old chap, very gentlemanly, with a kind, considerate face and was employed by the hospital to undertake odd jobs. Once he had tested whatever the appliance was, a small sticker was placed on the cord to say that this has been completed, presumably for fire and health and safety reasons.

One of my lesbian pals, admitted that she, prior to admission, had purchased the largest, blackest, re-chargeable vibrator known to man, courtesy of the Ann Summers catalogue. This huge obelisk, stood proud, and apparently when charging, the National Grid had to give clearance to increase output.

God knows what this little old man must have thought as he carried the zenith of manhood, with interchangeable heads, down the corridors of the hospital to his workshop to PAT test it. I did speak to someone who had seen him do this and he had to carry it over his shoulder due to the weight and size. Whilst doing so he was heard to be whistling the tune, 'Rabbit, Rabbit', by Chaz N Dave. Only one question remains:

'Where did he put the sticker?'

Another thing she shared with me was equally outrageous and will totally upset anyone God fearing.

(This book is starting to pan out that I will have virtually every pressure group of any description on my back if it is ever published and if so, so be it. Once again this is life, and we all find different things funny.

If you don't find some of the stories funny, or upset your fundamental ideologies and beliefs, I apologise. You have nearly finished reading the book anyway so I'll leave it up to you. I'm afraid this book is not, and never was intended for the faint hearted. However, if you are a regular church goer, please turn the page. I really would prefer you to! You have been warned!)

On my phone text box inwards was a rather amusing text joke based on the Lord's Prayer she sent me.

My vibrator, which brings me heaven,
Rabbit be thy name.
Till king dong come,
They make me cum on earth or is it heaven.
Give me this day my daily thrill,
And forgive me my screams
As I forgive those who sold me dud batteries.
Lead me straight into temptation
But deliver me from frustration
For thine is the vibration.
The power and rotation,
For ever, and ever
NO MEN

Now I play a little piano by ear. It certainly is not my first instrument of choice but I can bang out a few bits and bobs. Within the lounge was a rather expensive organ and yes it had been PAT tested and was black but didn't require the power that certain electrical items within the Priory needed to swell it and had far more buttons.

On it was a fantastic church organ sound and the instrument had foot pedals as found in many respected churches, for leading the choir and congregation alike. We found another of the Wine Glums who possessed a deep and soulful voice, to lead our service one Sunday, when we were really bored.

I played Jesu, Joy of Man's Desiring on the church organ voice, with a few growling base notes on the foot pedals, whilst he read out our Sunday prayer dedicated to our lesbian family members. I have to say that the congregation was a little sparse that day, comprising my two lesbian friends, the orator and me, however, we were overcome with the powerful message provided to us in all its majesty. And we all giggled a lot!

One of the Glums was actually evicted whilst I was in the nut house for the privileged. Bear in mind that the lounge was the meeting place for all the downstairs residents in the evenings, and other than on those nights that the addicts were being policed to AA meetings, it could become a busy old place. As I stated previously, it was a messy old room with biscuit wrappers adorning every glum sofa and coffee cups around the Wine Glums.

I couldn't understand why one of the Glums was there. She always appeared totally happy in life and had to involve herself in everybody else's problems. She was an out and out Geordie.

Now I love Geordies and have always found them to be fun, friendly and passionate people, the kind of people you would want to be mates with. Well, regrettably, this young lady was just a total pain in the arse. She knew everything about everyone and if she didn't she would either find out or make it up.

I think she must have been a dispensing chemist by trade, as she knew every pill's name and the group of pills to which it belonged. She also knew every dosage that should be administered and every herbal remedy which could be used as an alternative.

This pain of a 'Wy I Pet's' intelligence seemed to harbour a deep dichotomy. On one side she was clever, knowledgeable and wanted to be liked and liked everybody. On the other hand she must have had the brain of an amoeba, and possessed the tact of water buffalo. (Although I feel that this is a little unfair on our one-celled friend and hairy horny cows).

One evening, and probably not for the first time, rather than quaffing one of the glorious range of Brazilian coffees which were available from the free vending machine, she had chosen the largest mug from the communal kitchen and filled it with 1997 Chateau Neuf Du Pape. I'm sure it wasn't wine of this quality, but it's the only one I can think of.

As an aside, I once remember sitting next to a very posh gentleman on a plane from Manchester to Geneva, both of us travelling to skiing destinations. This was years ago and was during the time that I was sociable and could talk to people freely.

We started discussing fine wines which I knew nothing about whatsoever but wished to retain his attention in order that I could look at his wife's ample cleavage in the third seat of row G 1-3. He twittered on about how he had enjoyed many wine tasting holidays in France, Chile and Argentina and as I became bored rigid, I started undressing his wife's blouse in my mind, wondering what shape they would become upon release.

Her plumpcious norks, would they go downwards or sideways or both? Would her alveoli sprout hairs as long as the ones sprouting from her husband's ears? Would one be able to hang one's pakamac on her nipples if erect?

'Blah, blah, blah, blah,' went the husband. Ping went the front opening bra clasp with two of my fingers, amazingly dextrous in this regard from many a youthful fumble in the girls' six form common room.

Her heaving breasts momentarily pertened from the initial tightening of the clasp to explode in all their glory. Falling, falling with the weight of gravity towards her lap, her baps were not of the salt and pepper pot variety, but long and getting longer and longer by the nanosecond.

I mentally told myself to remember to write a letter of commendation to the brassiere manufacturer. How could two huge firm globes of delight be so liquid upon release? This was a 'wonder bra', a wondrous, wondrous bra.....

'What's your favourite wine?' Her husband brought me back to terra firma!

'Chateaubriand!' I replied in a confident manner, knowing that this chap would be mightily impressed with my knowledge of French wines and the Chateau from which they originated.

The conversation went very quiet after that and he too started to look at his wife's breasts. Who knows what was going through his mind! The love of them cling-filmed or the disappointment of them free. I couldn't understand why he had been distracted back to things he already knew so well and I asked my wife why he had suddenly gone so quiet.

'Chateaubriand steak is a recipe of a particular thick cut of the tenderloin, which according to Larousse Gastronomique, was created by personal chef

Monmireil, for Vincomte Francois-Rene de Chateaubriand (1768-1848) the author and diplomat who served Napolean as an Ambassador and Louis XV11 as Secretary of State for two years. The dish is usually offered as a serving for two persons as there is only enough meat in the centre of the average fillet for two portions!'

'Fuck right off!' I replied, knowing she had memorised the whole contents of Wikipedia.

'Obviously he didn't have more than one mate and I bet he drank it with Lambrini or Blue Nun'. Personally speaking, I would rather drink with a blue nun but this is a habitual trait passed down the ages.

Anyway, back to the tune army fan. This 'Why I luv ya pet and I'm sure ya luv me' amoeba had decided to bring the totally illegal liquid into the lounge. I walked through with a couple of visitors for a smoke out at the back in the garden and thought I was walking through the epicentre of the Stella Artois brewery factory.

Apparently, her boyfriend had brought her in sufficient quantities to enable her to switch codes (rugby language). She was summarily dismissed the next morning to contemplate her fate and future re-visit to the Priory. She was almost stoned to death by the Wine Glums. However, with the shakes comes the inability to hold a stone, never mind throw it.

There was another story dating back a few months that another woman had been evicted. Apparently she had asked her boy friend to drive to the car park at the rear of the building with two grams of cocaine. She was caught by a nurse, snorting the offending white powder via a ten pound note, in her pyjamas

And so to my eviction! On the 18th day the Lord said to me,

'Son, you are a total piss head and you always will be. Gird up your loins and go for the Glums for thine own comfort. You are not blessed with the fortitude to enter the Kingdom of AAdom and although I absolve you of all your sins, your deep unhappiness is born of the Devil incarnate. Only through divine intervention will you survive this beautiful world I have created for humanity and your glumness is truly profound.'

My Step One, mentioned earlier, had gone not so well in that it was quite obvious that I was not committed to giving up the dreaded liquor and to a degree I was only paying lip service. My depression had not improved one iota since arrival. The counsellors sought a meeting where one said that I was not ready to succumb to the Lord of AAdom and basically said I was wasting my time in my final week. The other did not want me to leave for my own safety. Bless her-I had thought she was a right grump as well!

I sought a meeting with my shrink. However this was Friday and he wasn't in until Monday, and was at Alton

Towers Theme Park that day and couldn't be contacted. The Nemesis of my depression had hit The Black Hole and following the Oblivion I had entered, I saw that the only option left available to me, was the Ripsaw. The Beastie has risen with a vengeance and I was heading for either The Dung Heap or The Squirrel Nutty Ride. So I settled down for a further weekend of unmitigated boredom at £625 per night but more importantly, reflected on the four days totally wasted of my maximum BUPA corporate coverage of 28 days.

On the Monday, first thing, it was agreed that I should move immediately to the Glums and sought solace late in the afternoon!!!! with the Glum project manager to provide me with a full and fulfilling programme of glum related therapies. However, he appeared to be rather glum.

'Off the record, Stephen, in the remaining seven days you have available through your corporate cover, I cannot put together a package where you will gain benefit. It would be far better to come back on an aftercare programme on a daily basis to optimise the time you have left.'

'Well whoopee, fucking whoopee doo!!!.'

Considering I was having suicidal intrusive thoughts on the Friday to be told I was to call back on a day basis over the next seven weeks was just what I needed to hear and cheered me up to the extent that following my discharge at 7.00 p.m. proceeded to the local off-licence for a bottle of gin, not of course, leaving Mr Schweppes out.

The shrink had to sign me out and I think he was rather reluctant to do so. I rather hoped that he would give me the address of the glum project manager in order that I could seek out an appropriate bow of an aged oak to hang from on the Tuesday morning.

'Blow me, Doreen, there's a man hanging from our tree. I thought I had pruned that branch last winter. Do you know, I think I know him, although his eyes don't look quite the same. They look a bit puffy and I am sure he is far redder than I remember.'

CHAPTER THIRTEEN:

So what do I do now?

Some things you must always be unable to bear –
William Faulkner

Our awesome responsibility to ourselves, to our children, and to the future is to create ourselves in the image of goodness, because the future depends on the nobility of our imaginings – Barbara Grizzuti Harrison

... it wasn't sin that was born on the day Eve picked an apple: what was born on that day was a splendid virtue called disobedience – Oriana Fellini

So we are nearly at the end of my rant and literary ramble and I hope that you have enjoyed reading some of the stories and anecdotes recounted in the book. I have thoroughly enjoyed writing it and I can now tick off another box in the things I wanted to do before I died.

I must start organising the next venture which is a threesome with Michelle Pfeiffer and Cheryl Cole. I gather that I am on Cheryl's list but Michelle may need some convincing as she doesn't fancy Cheryl.

Alternatively, I could write another book.

'Oh God, no!' I hear you all cry.

I could branch out and write a fiction thriller or maybe a reference book. How about tenth century persian pottery for example? I could combine the two and have a detective investigating the stealing of priceless artefacts. Somehow, I think not. I think it would be more appropriate to write a pornographic novel and have it serialised in Women's Weekly.

Music is such a huge part of my life that I must now finish my solo album which hopefully will be available for general release within the next four decades. I would also love to write a musical which would combine both writing and composing. I have already had some ideas about a teenage girl drug addict battling her addiction. Who knows?

Whatever I do, through recounting some of my past, it has helped me in resolving a few of my darkest feelings and fears, and that has to be a good thing. I continue to struggle with depression even following significant rehabilitation and whilst the world is not such a black place as it was six months ago, I am still very much affected by panic and anxiety attacks which are triggered in certain circumstances.

I think, once you 'own' a black dog, it never leaves your side and many psychologists state that you are susceptible to it all your life. This is also true of addiction and I suppose all who suffer from either have to learn how to cope with such a debilitating condition. Anyone reading the book who is affected by depression or any of its related illnesses, should not suffer in silence. It is an illness and don't let anyone tell you otherwise. You don't just snap out of it. It is easier to pass a camel than through the eye of a needle than change one's views voluntarily, believing life is truly wonderful and to be savoured. Google 'depression' and start to help yourself. It is an illness of the strong and don't let anyone tell you different.

Many with depression like to say they help others and are more concerned about others than themselves. But we must not forget that to help others *we* must be well and fit. A good analogy is like the safety talk on an aeroplane.

'Should pressure in the cabin fall, oxygen masks will appear from underneath the overhead lockers. For those with children, always ensure that your mask is fully fitted before attempting to fit those around you.'

How true this is in many aspects of life.

If you have been offended by any of the issues raised in this book, I am afraid I do not apologise. We all have our opinions. It is just that I have taken the time and trouble to write them on paper. I do not profess in spoken word and I certainly do not advocate that I speak on behalf of others.

I am my own man and I do not expect anyone to agree with me on anything. If I have struck a chord, whether good or bad, then that is good. It opens debate and gives a different slant on issues which many believe should not be spoken in public. For Heaven's sake, why not? Radical fundamentalists and dictators have openly pontificated about their views for hundreds of years. Give the voice back to the people; those law abiding, caring, ordinary folks who make up the vast majority of our population, for we have lost our voice. We are not brave enough and are fearful, living in a culture that castigates any person who speaks up against some issues deemed too 'sensitive' to be labelled.

I wish you all well and hope that you reap fulfilment, peace and harmony in life and just so that I don't have an unlucky thirteen chapters in my book......

CHAPTER FOURTEEN

Finis

The great thing in this world is not so much where we are, but in what direction we are moving – Oliver Wendell Holmes

Kindest regards.

Steve x

Contact Numbers and Help Sites:

The Samaritans:	www.**samaritans**.org/talk
Alcoholics Anonymous:	*www.**alcoholics-anonymous***
Cocaine Anonymous:	*www.cauk.org.uk*
Sex Addicts Anonymous:	stephensheardbooks.co.uk
Mind:	www.**mind**.org.uk
Child Line:	www.**childline**.org.uk/
Relate:	*www.**relate**.org.uk*

Steve Sheard can be contacted at

www.stephensheardbooks.co.uk

Made in the USA
Columbia, SC
21 November 2022